Looking
after your
Mental
Health

Edited by Felicity Brooks

With additional design by
Melissa Gandhi and Jenny Offley

Expert advice from:
Dr Louise Theodosiou,
Consultant Child Psychiatrist,
Spokesperson for the
Royal College of Psychiatrists, UK

Dr Jamie Lawler,
Assistant Professor of Psychology,
Eastern Michigan University

Katie Simon Phillips,
writer of mental health blog
www.bornwithoutmarbles.com

For links to websites with useful information on many of the
topics in this book, go to the Usborne Quicklinks website at
www.usborne.com/quicklinks, and type in the keywords 'mental
health'. Find out more on page 256.

Usborne Publishing Ltd., Usborne House, 83-85 Saffron Hill,
London EC1N 8RT, England. www.usborne.com
Printed in the UK. First published in 2018.
Copyright © 2018 Usborne Publishing Ltd. UKE.

Looking after your Mental Health

ALICE JAMES
& LOUIE STOWELL

Designed by Vickie Robinson

Illustrated by Nancy Leschnikoff
and Freya Harrison

CONTENTS

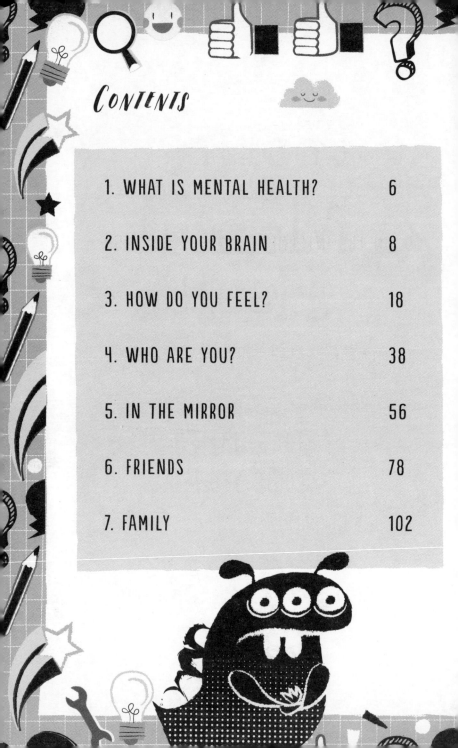

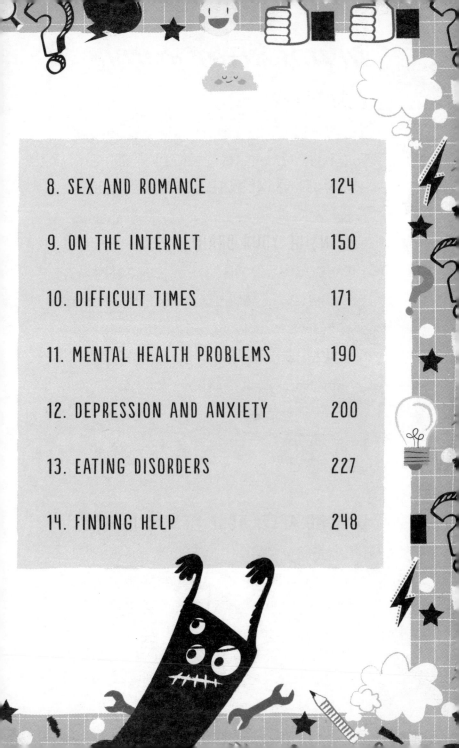

WHAT IS MENTAL HEALTH?

Your PHYSICAL HEALTH is the wellbeing of your body. It's something you're probably very aware of – you know your body can get hurt or become ill, and over time it usually heals and gets better.

But that's only one part of your wellbeing. Everyone also has MENTAL HEALTH – the state your brain is in, how it's feeling, thinking, and how it makes you behave.

Just like physical health, mental health changes throughout your life. Mental health can be good, just OK, or it can be poor and make you ill.

LOOKING AFTER YOUR MENTAL HEALTH

It's really important to look after your mental health, especially as you get older and your emotions become busier and more intense, and there's more pressure on you at school and home.

You probably know how to look after your physical health (eat broccoli, wash your hands, don't jump out of moving vehicles, and so on), but it's harder to know how to look after your mental health.

This book is designed to help you navigate some of the challenges that might affect your mental health. It includes challenges everyone faces, from problems with friends and family, exams and social media, to less common, serious mental health conditions such as depression and anxiety.

INSIDE YOUR BRAIN

WHAT DO BRAINS DO?

Your brain is your body's control centre – it's in charge of almost everything you do, and it processes information from all of your senses, to help you understand the world. Here are just some of the things your brain does on a daily basis:

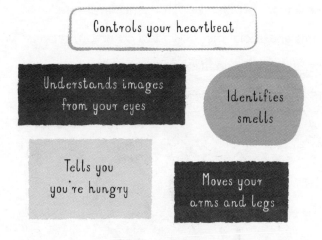

Controls your heartbeat

Understands images from your eyes

Identifies smells

Tells you you're hungry

Moves your arms and legs

It does all of those things automatically – without you even realizing.

THE IMPORTANT PART

Your brain has one more, very important ability,
an ability you probably associate with your brain
more than smelling stuff or moving you about.
It can think.

Every minute of every day your brain
is thinking – wondering, remembering,
daydreaming and feeling.

Thoughts

WHERE DO FEELINGS COME FROM?

Feelings, or emotions, are caused by chemical messengers in your brain called hormones and neurotransmitters. Happiness, sadness, excitement, anger – they're all caused by chemistry.

HORMONES are released into your blood and travel around your body. Here are three important ones, the emotions they trigger and what they do:

ADRENALINE

FEAR, ANXIETY, ANGER

Makes connections in your brain fire really quickly, sending messages around your body very fast to get it ready for action.

OXYTOCIN

LOVE, TRUST, SYMPATHY

Released when someone hugs you or holds your hand, especially when you're little. It calms your whole body down and makes you feel relaxed and loved.

CORTISOL

STRESS

Helps your body deal with stressful situations, by reducing sensitivity to pain, increasing energy in the muscles, and improving memory.

NEUROTRANSMITTERS help cells in your brain communicate with one another. Here are the main two that affect how you feel:

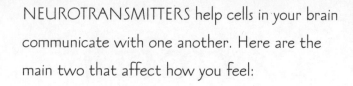
Serotonin

HAPPINESS, SADNESS

Controls all your moods. The right amount keeps you happy, but not enough of it might make you feel sad or depressed.

DOPAMINE

PRIDE, EXCITEMENT

Part of something called a reward pathway - it makes you want to do things to get a reward, and makes you feel pleased when you do something well.

Exactly how you feel depends on the different chemicals firing through your brain.

WHY DO WE HAVE EMOTIONS?

Emotions can be painful – being angry or upset is usually unpleasant. But emotions exist for a reason, and do a very important job – they help people survive. This was especially important thousands of years ago.

Disgust stops you from eating or touching things that could be infectious, or give you diseases.

Love helps you form relationships and raise children.

Fear gets your body ready for fighting or running away, so you don't get hurt.

Your brain and body are linked up, and intense emotions can cause physical responses in your body. For example, if you're very scared your heart beats faster, and you might get sweaty or shaky hands – that's the hormone noradrenaline getting your body ready to flee or tackle a dangerous situation.

Emotions also strengthen your bonds with other people. Humans are very social, and showing emotions outwardly helps everyone to understand each other. The expressions that show on our faces are the same all over the world – they don't depend on language or culture.

DIFFERENT BRAINS

During puberty your brain gets rewired, forming
a network of connections you'll have through
your life. This is just part of getting you ready
to be an adult — you're not going to completely
change personality, or wake up one day a
different person. You might just notice you feel
emotions more intensely, and often at the same
time. Everyone's brain is slightly different, so it's
normal not to feel the same as other people,
even in the same situations.

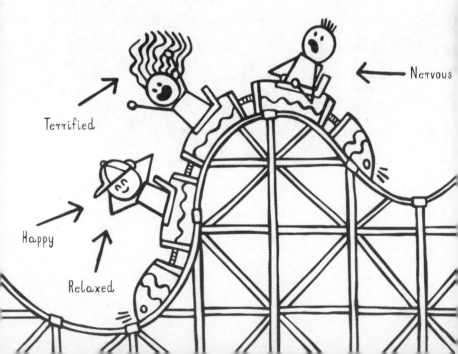

Terrified

Nervous

Happy

Relaxed

THE POWER OF SLEEP

One of the most important things your brain needs is sleep.

When you are asleep, your body slows down but your brain keeps going. It uses the time to process information, make memories, and even clear out waste that builds up in the day. You need extra sleep during puberty, while your body changes and develops, and your brain forms lots of new connections.

If you can't sleep, don't worry. Worrying about whether you've got enough sleep doesn't help, but each hour of sleep you get will do you good.

TRY THIS...

- Have a shower or bath before getting into bed. The warm water relaxes your muscles, and as you cool down afterwards, your body's processes slow down and you feel calm.

- Keep phones, laptops and tablets out of bed. The bright light stimulates your brain, making it harder to relax.

- Light exercise is great for a better night's sleep, but don't exercise too close to bedtime or it'll take longer to wind down.

- If you're thinking about a lot of different things and struggling to relax, try writing down some of your thoughts, such as things you have to do or ideas you have. Then you can forget about them until the morning.

- Try to stick to a similar routine, even at weekends. This helps your brain and body know when to shut off and when to kickstart again.

3

How do you FEEL?

MOODSPOTTING

If you were blissfully happy all the time, you would never need to think about your feelings or put them into words. (If you did, those words wouldn't make very interesting reading.)

Dear Diary,

Today I feel happy. As I did yesterday. And the day before. I will probably be happy tomorrow. Do I actually need to fill in any more days?

But even happy people feel bad sometimes, and learning how to identify and name your emotions can be very helpful.

Once you know what *kind* of badness you're feeling, you'll be in a better position to make yourself feel better.

It can be surprisingly hard to put your feelings into words. Sometimes, looking at a list of feelings can help you pinpoint your mood.

Do any of these feelings match how you're feeling right now? Or perhaps a combination of several?

Angry

Determined

Sociable

Arrogant

Ill

Optimistic

Bored

Shocked

Curious

Worried

Silly

Frightened

Confident

Unsure

Happy

THE BIG ONES

Most emotions are variations on a few, powerful feelings, such as happiness and sadness, fear and anger. We use words like 'happy' all the time. But what *is* happiness? And what is sadness?

1. HAPPINESS

Happiness has lots of variations, but it's always a positive emotion: it makes you feel good. You may experience happiness differently from someone else. There's no right way to feel it.

It can be a really strong feeling that floods you completely, as though you're being filled up with hot light. That kind of happiness is also known as joy or euphoria.

Happiness can also be a calmer feeling, like a little glow inside your chest, called contentment.

I'M NOT HAPPY. WHAT'S WRONG WITH ME?

Nothing. Happiness isn't something you're likely to feel all the time, or even most of the time.

Not being happy all the time doesn't mean you have a bad life, it just means you're human. Part of the meaning and excitement of human existence comes from having to struggle and overcome problems.

I can do it...I can do it...I...ouch, stitch...I can do it...

HAPPY SCIENCE

For an emotion that feels simple, happiness has a
complex web of chemical activity behind it,
and scientists don't fully understand its causes.
But here are some of the chemicals involved in happiness:

OXYTOCIN

Serotonin

DOPAMINE

And…**ENDORPHINS.** These chemicals are part of your
body's painkilling system. Exercise releases endorphins, which
is one of the reasons exercising can be good for your mood.

For more information on these hormones and
neurotransmitters turn back to pages 10–12.

2. SADNESS

Like happiness, feeling bad comes in many forms.
Sadness can be like a whisper, a tiny sense that
something isn't quite right. Or it can mean
feeling so miserable that you burst into noisy
tears in front of everyone.

Often, sadness comes when something in
your life goes wrong – from someone being rude
to you to a death in the family. It can also come
and go for no particular reason.

WHY DO WE CRY?

Tears have a couple of physical jobs to do. For a start, they keep your eyes moist. They also help you blink away dust, or flush out poisons, such as the irritating chemical given off when you chop onions. But emotional tears are more complicated.

There are a few different theories as to why humans cry in response to emotions. One is that crying lets an aggressive person know that you're not a threat – a little like the way dogs roll on their backs to show they're submissive to bigger dogs. Another theory is that crying signals to others that you're vulnerable and need help.

Whatever the reason, emotional tears have a different chemical structure from other kinds of tears. So, in theory, a scientist could tell if you're lying about having 'something in your eye' while watching a sad film.

3. ANGER

Anger can feel like a fire inside your chest. It can burst out as though from nowhere, or it can simmer for a long time like a pan of water that eventually boils over.

Anger is one of those feelings you're often told not to feel. It's seen as bad and dangerous, even though, in itself, there's nothing wrong with it. Anger is only harmful if you act on it thoughtlessly, as you might end up doing something you regret once you've calmed down.

Just feeling angry isn't bad in itself. In fact, it can be useful. Anger can give you the motivation to change your situation, and it might help you to realize that something is going wrong in a friendship, warning you to do something about it.

Anger is only a problem when you don't deal with it properly.

There are some suggestions about how to deal with anger in positive ways on pages 110-111.

THE SCIENCE OF ANGER

Anger starts in a part of your brain called the amygdala, which sends messages to your adrenal glands (which are on top of your kidneys). Before you know it, adrenaline is pumping through you, giving you that hot, ultra-alert feeling that comes with anger. Anger also makes you produce more of a hormone called testosterone, which can make you feel as though you want to fight.

Anger changes your face, tensing your muscles and making you scowl. You might also start to talk more quickly and loudly. These external signs of anger are a sign to others to tread carefully.

4. FEAR

When you're afraid, your heart beats faster and your muscles tense. You might feel both hot and cold at the same time.

In dangerous situations, fear can help you survive, getting your muscles ready to run or fight. Even imagined danger can prompt those responses – fear is your body's alarm system, and it gets your body ready to deal with danger.

You might also feel afraid before a test, or an awkward conversation - people often feel fear in situations where there's not even a hint of physical danger.

That shadow on my bedroom wall is DEFINITELY a werewolf and not a dressing gown.

Sometimes, this fear can help motivate you – for example, it might make you revise for that test – but it can also get in the way. Sometimes, fear almost seems to paralyse you, making it hard to do or say (or write) anything.

WHY DOES THIS HAPPEN?

Freezing on the spot when you're scared seems unhelpful, but it might relate to when humans had to deal with a lot of predators. There are some predators who are more likely to notice you when you move, so staying still can be a good survival tactic. It doesn't work as well when you're sitting an exam, sadly.

5. SURPRISE

When something unexpected happens, you feel surprise. It's like a little jolt through your body. Sometimes, if it's a nasty surprise, it can feel like fear. Often, though, surprise is a positive emotion. It can give you a sudden rush of happiness. (Many emotions are interconnected – feeling one might lead to feeling another.)

6. EXCITEMENT

Excitement is a feeling that often looks to the future. People get excited when something good is about to happen, for example, the day before going on holiday. It's connected to happiness and to hope – feeling positive about the future.

You can feel excited about the present, for example if you're talking about a topic you're obsessed with to someone else who loves talking about it.

7. EMBARRASSMENT

Embarrassment is an emotion that you feel in relation to other people. It's a feeling you get when you think you've done something wrong or foolish, and other people have noticed. It can make your face feel hot, and some people blush.

You're more likely to get embarrassed if you care what other people think of you. It's a feeling you're likely to experience less intensely as you get older, so you can look forward to an old(er) age of doing whatever you feel like, and embarrassing your younger relatives.

One way to cope with embarrassment is to ask yourself whether anyone actually minds. Does falling over in public, or wearing your clothes inside out change what people think or feel about you? Would you mind if it happened to somebody else?

8. ENVY AND JEALOUSY

They are different feelings, but closely linked. Envy is when you want something someone else has, such as a new phone. Jealousy is when you fear someone else is going to ruin something you have – often a relationship. Both emotions can spoil otherwise good situations. These feelings tend to get better if you talk about them. Often, they're based on misunderstandings and assumptions.

I wish she was MY best friend.

What if she stops being my best friend now that girl's around?

Dum di dum di dum I have no idea that they're feeling anything other than happy to be my friend because they haven't actually said anything.

Envy and jealousy have a role to play in forming strong relationships. Feeling jealous is a reminder that a person matters to you and it motivates you to pay attention to them.

9. LONELINESS

Loneliness is a cold, sad feeling. It's a little like hunger, only in your mind. Just as your stomach rumbles when you need food, loneliness could be your mind telling you you need company.

Being alone doesn't necessarily mean you're lonely – and a lot of people enjoy having alone time. You also don't have to be alone to feel lonely. In fact, feeling lonely when you're around other people can be the worst kind of loneliness. Sometimes loneliness is about feeling as though you don't fit in with a particular group of people, or that a relationship isn't working.

Loneliness can pass on its own. At other times, making new friends might be the answer.

10. LOVE

Love comes in many varieties, from family love to friend love and romantic love, or even the love you might feel for a fictional character.

Like happiness, it can be very intense, or a slow, warm feeling that hums in the background of your life. Love can be a glue between people, but it can also hurt a lot if the person you love doesn't feel the same way or treats you badly. As with happiness, the hormone oxytocin plays a role in creating feelings of love.

11. HATRED

The flipside of love is hatred. Sometimes, the two feelings can be very close together, as both are intense, and both relate to people who have a big impact on your life. You could think of hatred as love's fiery evil twin.

FEELINGS AREN'T FIXED

Feelings change often and quickly. Sometimes, feelings are related to what's going on in your life in that moment. At other times, it can be harder to pin down where your feelings are coming from. Whatever you're feeling in this moment, it isn't forever. Feelings are temporary, and they ebb and flow over time.

IMPORTANT: all feelings are OK, even bad ones – a bad feeling doesn't make you a bad person. What you have to do is learn how to react to your feelings, and be gentle with yourself. Bad feelings can be your mind telling you something is wrong, giving you a chance to put it right. For example, if you're angry with a friend, that anger is a chance to talk to them and find a way to make up. Often bad feelings are fleeting, and go away on their own, given time.

NAME IT TO TAME IT

One good reason for trying to work out what you're feeling is that it can actually help you change your mood. Working out what you're feeling can help you get some distance from those feelings, so they're not as overwhelming. Sometimes, just giving a feeling a name can help it start to float away or dissolve.

Not all emotions can be named in every language. Some highly specific emotions only exist in certain languages. For example:

- SUKHA (SANSKRIT) – genuine lasting happiness that doesn't depend on the circumstances.
- SHINRIN-YOKU (JAPANESE) – the relaxation you feel when bathing in the forest.
- TARAB (ARABIC) – a state of ecstasy or enchantment caused by music.

TRY THIS...

Keep a mood journal for a few days. You don't have to write much. You could just note down the date, what you were feeling, and what was happening that day. Do you notice any patterns? Do any feelings come up a lot?

You could lay out your journal like this:

DATE: Monday 2nd June

FEELING: Lonely and angry

WHAT HAPPENED?
Had an argument with my sister.

WHAT ELSE IS ON MY MIND?
Have a test tomorrow at school.

ACTION: I went upstairs and read.

HOW DID I FEEL AN HOUR LATER?
Felt a bit better after reading and went and watched TV with sister.

4

WHO ARE YOU?

FINDING YOUR IDENTITY

When you're born, you don't really have a distinct sense of yourself. It's not until the age of about three that children start thinking of themselves as individuals with their own unique qualities and tastes.

The world is me. Bow before me, world, for all rises and falls at my command.

I'm three years old and I have a dog and I don't like cheese and I have brown eyes.

Your sense of self develops with age, and as you get older you're likely to ask more and more questions about what it means to be you. Your sense of self is known as your identity.

Discovering who you are and shaping that identity takes time, and it is a process that doesn't stop. Most people's identity changes and develops all through their lives.

FEELING PHILOSOPHICAL

Philosophers – people who specialize in thinking about the big questions of life – have puzzled over the question of identity for thousands of years. Philosophers ask questions such as:

- "What does it mean to be a person?"
- "Am I the person I was last year? Or even five minutes ago?"
- "Do I have a soul?"

Growing up involves thinking like a philosopher about yourself (and the world). Things that seem obvious when you're small start to shift and change, especially during puberty.

39

BECOMING YOU

Although your identity shifts all through your life, some of the biggest changes will come during and just after puberty. Your body changes shape and size, while your brain forms new connections and pumps out hormones that change the way you feel. But beyond the physical and mental changes, you're likely to be starting a new school and making decisions about what to study, what to spend your time doing, who to be friends with, and what type of adult you want to become. This can be very stressful.

CHOOSE FROM THE FOLLOWING OPTIONS:

HISTORY ☐
GEOGRAPHY ☐
FRENCH ☐
NOT HAVING TO MAKE ANY MORE
IMPORTANT DECISIONS TODAY PLEASE ☑

TRYING ON IDENTITIES

It can be a confusing time, but puberty, and the teenage years as a whole, can also be exciting. It's a chance to experiment with who you are – to dress differently, to listen to all styles of music, to make friends with lots of different people, and find new ways of expressing yourself.

Few people make it through adolescence without writing some moody poetry or stories. If you have not written any poetry about the darkness of your soul yet, don't worry. You will.

A WORK IN PROGRESS

As you puzzle over your identity, you may feel uncertain and scared. That's normal. It's OK not to have everything worked out. Becoming you takes time.

If you ever find life confusing or overwhelming, it can be very calming to simply tell yourself that everything is OK. Try repeating it silently to yourself. It's oddly calming, even at times when you don't fully believe it.

FITTING IN AND STANDING OUT

An important part of finding out more about your identity is working out how you fit in with other people. The need to belong is a powerful human urge, but so is the desire to be special and unique. Learning to balance those two things can be difficult, especially in places such as school.

We are all individuals!

The pressure to wear or do certain things can be strong, but it's worth remembering that everyone else is as full of doubts as you are. Everyone's just trying to work out where they fit in (while trying to feel individual, too). There's more about peer pressure on pages 90-91.

WHAT MATTERS MOST TO YOU?

Whatever people around you think is important,
you need to decide what matters to you.
Ask yourself...

- What do you think is important in life?
- What are the things you would stand up for even if
  everyone else were against them?
- What does it mean to be a good person?

Your answers may well change all through
your life, but it's important to have a sense of
what you value.

That's not to say you should think your
opinions are the only ones that matter; not at all.
It's just that knowing what you care about can
help to protect you in difficult times, because it
reminds you that the world is important and full
of things worth fighting for.

SELF-ESTEEM

Self-esteem is the opinion we have of ourselves. High self-esteem doesn't mean thinking you're the greatest human in the history of the planet. It just means believing that you're important and worthwhile (which you are). Holding on to that belief can be difficult when life is turbulent.

There are more tips for boosting your self-esteem on pages 50-51, but here's one thing to try if you ever start feeling bad about yourself:

Ask yourself what you'd say to a friend who was feeling bad. If your friend said "I'm worthless", you'd disagree with this and probably say they were great and wonderful, so why not treat yourself with the same kindness? Try to be a friend to yourself.

LOW SELF-ESTEEM

Occasional feelings of guilt or shame, when you do something bad, are just part of life, but sometimes those feelings can mutate into something harder to shake off. Feeling that you're a fundamentally bad person, or worthless, or a failure, isn't something you should just have to put up with. Listen out for negative thoughts and try to counter them with positive ones.

I'm worthless.

NEGATIVE AND POSITIVE SELF-TALK

'Self-talk' is the way you talk to yourself in your own head. Instead of saying, "I'm no good", try saying, "I'm good. I matter." It sounds incredibly cheesy, but it can make you feel better, especially if you keep telling yourself positive things whenever a negative thought pops up.

No, I matter!

If the negative thoughts are very loud, or frequent, talk to an adult about them.

DON'T COMPARE

It's easy to look at someone else and think that they're leading an amazing, charmed life.

Yes, some lucky people breeze through life without many doubts, but most people work hard to project confidence. Although someone can seem to have it together on the outside, they're often struggling underneath in ways you can't see.

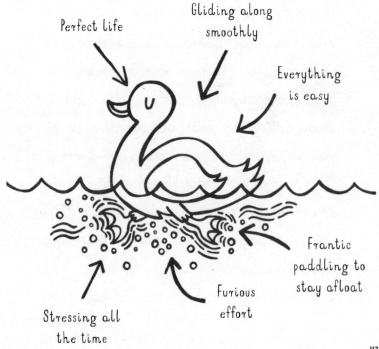

Perfect life

Gliding along smoothly

Everything is easy

Frantic paddling to stay afloat

Furious effort

Stressing all the time

IMAGINARY AUDIENCE

You might feel self-conscious when you're at school, or out and about, and feel that everyone is looking at you, and noticing flaws you think you have in your appearance or personality. This is really common, and is known as an imaginary audience.

Though it might feel as if everyone's looking at you and judging you, in reality, everyone is so busy getting on with their own lives and conquering their own worries that no one notices that spot on your forehead, the toothpaste on your trousers or your odd socks. It's natural to worry about how other people see you, but try not to get too bogged down by it.

You are much more likely to spot the good things about someone else than the bad things, and other people are doing the same with you.

What you think people are thinking:

What people are actually thinking:

I wonder what's for lunch today?

His top doesn't fit very well.

He looks kind of spotty today.

Only 67 days until my birthday.

His hair is really greasy.

If I had a pet gorilla, I'd call him Charles.

49

TRY THIS...

Here are a few things you can do to boost your confidence and self-esteem.

1. Don't compare yourself to others.

A human being isn't like homework that you can copy. Everyone is different, and your own experiences and achievements are special and unique. (Also, don't copy homework. Being told off by teachers isn't good for your self-esteem.)

2. Set yourself small goals (as well as long-term ones).

Whether it's baking a cake or tidying your room, setting yourself small, achievable goals every day can have a really positive effect on your confidence, because it's a daily reminder that you can achieve things. Plus, your brain is set up to reward you when you get stuff done — it's part of a system called a reward pathway. Your brain releases a pleasurable chemical called dopamine when you achieve something, which makes you feel good.

3. Give yourself credit.

Remember to pat yourself on the back when you've done something good. It's all too easy to move on and discount past achievements, worrying about the future. Take time to think "I did that well".

4. Allow yourself to make mistakes.

Trying something new can often mean getting things wrong. That's a good thing. Allowing yourself to do things badly is part of the learning process. If you can't do something first time around, that doesn't mean you're bad at it. It's just the first step to being good at something.

GENDER IDENTITY

Your relationship with something called gender has a big effect on your sense of yourself. Using scans before birth, or at birth, doctors find out what *sex* a baby is – whether it's a boy, a girl, or (more rarely) a mix, which is known as being intersex. ('Inter' is Latin for between.)

Being intersex usually means having a mix of male and female physical sex organs, such as a penis and also ovaries.

Simply put, sex is about what type of body you're born with. gender is more complicated.

You could think of sex as the physical side of things – which body parts you have, for example – but gender is more about who you are and how you see yourself, as well as what people expect of you. Gender expectations can start making themselves felt at a very young age.

Different societies have different expectations in relation to gender. These expectations can be tough to deal with, and put a lot of pressure on you. Ideas of what makes 'a real man' or 'a real woman' are forced on all of us all the time, by the media and by the world in general. The weight of all these expectations can be hard to bear, especially if you don't conform to gender stereotypes.

GENDER DYSPHORIA

Some people feel that their gender identity doesn't match the sex assigned to them at birth. For example, someone whose sex is assigned at birth as male, may not identify as a boy, or man. This is sometimes known as being trans or transgender.

If your gender identity matches your physical sex, then that's known as being cis or cisgender. Other people don't fall neatly into either a male or a female gender identity. They might identify as genderfluid, or genderqueer.

Some trans people will decide to change their bodies to fit their gender identity better, taking hormones and having surgery. This is sometimes known as transitioning.

SEXUALITY

As you approach puberty, or even earlier, you might start having romantic or sexual thoughts and feelings for other people. The thoughts might be about people of a different sex, or the same sex as you, or both... or you might not have any at all. All these things are normal. Discovering your sexual identity, or sexuality, takes time, and your feelings may change throughout your life. (There's a lot more about sex and romance in Chapter 8.)

GROWING UP CAN BE SLOW

Knowing who you are is a process. You don't just wake up one morning with your identity fully formed. Even adults are still working out who they are. Many adults still feel like children pretending to be grown-ups, somehow getting away with being able to run their own lives...

5

IN THE MIRROR

THERE IS NO NORMAL

It can be a struggle to love your body. We are constantly bombarded with messages saying that, to live a happy life, you need a perfect body.

Bodies come in many, many shapes and sizes. Just looking around you in the street can tell you that. This isn't to say you should try to compare yourself to other people; it's just that being aware of the variety of bodies out there is a good reminder that no two people are the same, and that there's no right way to look.

Things normal bodies might have: scars, hair, cellulite, wrinkles, asymmetry (not matching on both sides), bent bits, missing bits, extra bits, big bits, small bits, wobbly bits, knobbly bits. Everything is OK.

BODY IMAGE

The way you feel about your own body is known as your body image. Some people think they look great, but for a lot of people, especially during puberty, maintaining a positive body image is hard work. It's normal to have the odd negative thought about your body, but if you find it happens a lot, there are lots of things in this chapter that you can try, to improve your body image.

Insecurity about your body feels a bit like this.

GROWING AND CHANGING

You've been growing all your life, but during puberty, that speeds up. Not only are you likely to grow taller, you might get bigger all over, and look less like a child, and more like an adult. This can be unsettling, even if you're eager to leave childhood behind, as all big changes can take some getting used to. Or you might feel that you're not changing quickly enough, and you want to be taller, or generally more grown-up looking. Some people don't want puberty to start, and don't want to leave childhood behind – that's normal too.

Everyone starts developing at different times, and develops at different rates. For a while you might find yourself feeling awkward and out of touch with your body. That happens to a lot of people, and if you feel that way you're not alone. Give yourself time to get to know your new shape, and be comfortable in it.

It might feel like a shock to start with, but you'll get used to it.

Throughout history, across the world, people have found all sorts of different things attractive.

For example:

- In Renaissance Italy the most beautiful women were full-figured, with rounded bodies and large hips.
- In the 1700s in France, King Louis XVI made it fashionable for men to have elaborate hairstyles, and wear lots of make-up, heels, and luxurious clothes.
- For many centuries, in India and other countries around the world, being fat or overweight was desirable, because it showed you were wealthy and able to buy lots of food.
- In 1920s America, women wanted straight figures with slender hips and flat chests.

SPEAK KINDLY

The words you use to describe
your body can shape how you think
about it. A good habit to get into is to focus
on saying kind things about your body, whether
that's out loud or just in your head. If the urge
to say something negative pops up, try this...

OUT LOUD?

If you're in a situation where other people are moaning
about their bodies, you don't have to join in and say
anything bad about yours. You could just wait until the
topic moves on, or better still, say something nice
about someone else.

IN YOUR HEAD?

If you catch yourself saying something negative in your head, reply by giving yourself a compliment. Think of it a little like having an argument with yourself, but an argument that you win by being nice. If the negative voice says something mean, say something kind instead.

SHHH, ADULTS!

If the adults in your life say negative things about their own bodies in front of you, politely ask them not to. It's easy to pick up signals from the world around you that affect your own body image, and if the adults in your life are always going on about how fat/ugly/old/short/bald they are, that can seep into your brain.

BODY IMAGE AND FOOD

Feeding your body properly is an important part of treating your body kindly. Food gives you the energy you need to do all the things you want in life, and helps keep your body healthy.

On top of that, food is part of many of the good things in life, from birthday parties to sharing lunch with a friend. In many cultures, today and in the past, sharing food is a sign of trust, celebration and welcome.

People with a poor body image may develop a complicated relationship with food. In some cases, this can become an eating disorder – a mental health problem that affects how much and what they eat.

> You can find out more about eating disorders in Chapter 13.

HEALTHY EATING

One part of healthy eating is making
sure that when you're hungry, you eat a
wide range of foods, especially:

- Carbohydrates, such as potatoes, pasta, rice
  and grains
- Proteins, such as fish, cheese, meat or tofu
- Fruit and vegetables, in a range of colours
- Dairy, such as milk, yogurt and cheese

You've probably heard advice like this a million
times, but what you eat is only half of the picture.
What happens in your mind when you eat is also
very important. Even if you eat a very balanced
diet, with lots of variety, if you feel upset or
guilty while you eat, it isn't healthy.

You deserve to feed your body a wide variety
of foods without feeling bad about it.

DAMAGING DIETS

The word 'diet' can mean 'all the things you eat in your daily life'. It can also refer to a medically recommended diet, which means a doctor has suggested eating particular foods to help with medical problems.

Usually, though, when someone says, "I'm going on a diet", they mean they're restricting the amount or type of food they eat to try to lose weight. If you are advised by a doctor that you are overweight, and need to lose weight for your health, then follow the advice to become healthier. But if you are not overweight, weight loss diets can be very harmful for your body and mind.

Here are just a few of the problems they
can cause:

- Some diets involve not eating certain types of food which might mean you miss out on important nutrients that you need to stay healthy. During puberty, you're growing and developing, and you need to eat all kinds of foods to make sure your brain and body get what they need.

- Weight-gain diets, for people trying to 'bulk' or gain muscle mass can be just as unhealthy. Just eating protein, or protein supplement drinks, is an unbalanced, unhealthy diet that can cause long-term problems.

- Sometimes talking lots about weight loss diets can affect the people around you, and make them feel like they should be on diets too. If a doctor has recommended that you diet for your health, you can talk about it, but it's still a good idea to be sensitive to people around you. Some people don't have a very good relationship with food, and hearing other people talking about dieting can be upsetting.

- Dieting can affect your mood and thoughts. Not eating enough can make you irritable and make your head feel cloudy and vague.

USING YOUR BODY

As well as having a healthy relationship with food, another important part of having a positive body image is keeping healthy by using your body in ways that feel good.

That doesn't have to mean becoming a star footballer or running for miles. It's about doing active things that you enjoy, that get your blood pumping faster and your muscles working. Maybe you like social things, such as football or netball or dancing. Or you might prefer going for a quiet bike ride or a walk. Or perhaps something relaxing like swimming or yoga suits you best.

BODY AND MIND

Activities such as yoga can be very
helpful for your mental health,
as they work your mind
and body together.

In the short-term, all physical activity can
help put you in a better mood, as it creates
endorphins (see page 12). In the long-term,
doing things that help you appreciate what your
body can do, rather than what it looks like, is
good for your body image.

SOCIAL MEDIA

One thing that can get in the way of you having a healthy relationship with your body is the little box of people and pictures in your pocket. Having social media apps on your phone means it's easy to constantly compare yourself to others.

Chapter 9 is all about using social media in a way that doesn't have a negative impact on your mental health.

One very important thing you can do for yourself is take a break from social media. You don't have to like every picture or even look at any of them. You don't have to be available online all the time. It's OK to take time offline.

THE MEDIA

Beyond social media, we get a lot of messages about what bodies should look like – from films, websites and blogs, magazines, adverts and TV shows.

"PERFECT" STAR HAS SLIGHT IMPERFECTION ON HER BODY. THE HORROR.

TEN WAYS TO MAKE YOUR MUSCLES BIGGER THAN YOUR HEAD.

HOW DARE THIS POP STAR GO ON HOLIDAY WITHOUT STOMACH MUSCLES THAT LOOK LIKE THEY'VE BEEN CARVED OUT OF MARBLE!

We're used to seeing models and actors with unusually thin, shapely or muscular bodies as the 'norm', because that's what's on TV and in films most of the time. These are people who are paid to look a certain way.

Most celebrities don't actually look like the pictures of themselves when they aren't wearing lots of make-up, and the lighting is less flattering. Techniques such as digital image manipulation are also used – using computers to make people in photographs look taller or thinner or more muscular or handsome.

Films don't literally tell the audience, "This is what you should look like". But by only showing 'perfect' bodies and faces, they get you used to looking at that type of body, and it's easy to see it as normal, when really it's not. So, what should you do about it?

QUESTION EVERYTHING

Learn to be a sceptical viewer. When you see
an advert featuring someone handsome, athletic
or beautiful, don't just take it at face value.
Think about the hours they probably spent
in the make-up chair, working out, dieting
dangerously, or even having plastic surgery.

Remember: when someone is trying to sell
you something, making you feel good *the way
you are* isn't in their best interests. They want
you to think you have a problem that can be
fixed with their product, to make money out
of you.

BUY ME!

YOU WILL LOOK LIKE THIS ACTOR EVEN
THOUGH HE ONLY LOOKS LIKE THIS
BECAUSE WE DREW ON HIS ABDOMINAL
MUSCLES DIGITALLY AND HE HAS
PROBABLY NEVER USED THIS PRODUCT.

FORM A REBEL ALLIANCE

Building a positive body image takes time, especially because society so often throws messages at you that are designed to make you unhappy with your body. You need to learn to be a rebel in that sense, but it's easier to resist the unhelpful messages society puts out when you have allies. If you find out that your friends are struggling with body image problems, or want to stay feeling positive about themselves, you could make a pact not to criticize your own bodies. If you compliment one another, accept those compliments and try not to reject them.

I think you look great today.

Why, thank you! I thought so too...

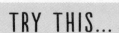

TRY THIS...

Telling yourself you are worthwhile and your body is beautiful and wonderful can be difficult and embarrassing. You might not know what to say, so here are some things you could tell yourself. Positive statements like this are known as affirmations. (They might sound cheesy, but you can blame us for that.)

I'm not an object to be looked at. I'm a person looking out at the world.

I respect and love my body.

I am OK. Everything is OK. My body is OK, exactly as it is.

My value has nothing to do with the size and shape of my body, or my face.

You could also try some of these activities to boost your body confidence:

- Make a list of things you like about your body.
- Try an activity that's a little out of your comfort zone, perhaps badminton, belly dancing or a clowning workshop.
- Hug someone. Physical contact is important and releases happy chemicals in your brain.
- Wear comfortable clothes that fit you well and feel nice against your skin.
- Spend time outdoors.
- Rest when you're tired. Lying down on the sofa and reading a book is just as valuable a thing to do with your body as going for a run.

'Make a list of things you
like about your body.'

Some people find this one really, really hard. If
complimenting yourself feels like a big challenge,
start small:

My eyes are a nice colour.
My feet are good because
they help me walk.

It's better to think of something small or even silly,
than to avoid thinking of good things altogether.

If your body image is very negative, and
you find yourself almost constantly having bad
thoughts about how you look, it might help
to speak to someone. You could start with a
teacher or counsellor at your school, or a parent
or carer who may be able to talk it through
with you and help you.

Occasionally, really negative body image
turns into a more serious problem.
Read more from page 227.

6

FRIENDS

CAVE FRIENDS

For early humans, friendship was essential for survival – groups of humans had to work together to stay safe and find enough food to eat. Working in groups is easier and more effective when people have an emotional bond.

Your relationship with your friends probably isn't a matter of life and death now, but if a friend says something hurtful, or you are left out of a group, it can stir up some powerful negative feelings.

Friends can have an amazingly positive impact on your life and your mental health, too.

WHAT ARE FRIENDS FOR?

Friendships are some of the most important relationships you'll ever have. Good friends can help you, support you, make you laugh, stop you doing stupid things, and congratulate you when you do great things.

CONGRATULATIONS

Hooray for friends!

Yay!

FRIENDSHIP GIVES YOU...

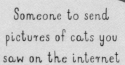

Loads of happy memories

Someone to send pictures of cats you saw on the internet

A sense of belonging

Helpless laughter

Better health – lots of scientific studies suggest that having close friends means you'll live longer

Someone to share good news with

Woof!
Woof!
Woof!

Someone to talk to about worries you have

Help coping with big life events

HOW MANY FRIENDS IS ENOUGH?

The quality of friendships is much more important than the quantity. Having just a few, close friends, will give you all the support you need, and probably help you more than a vast network of shallow friendships, including friends on social media.

Even if you have hundreds of people you could say hello to at a party or online, there might not be many people who you can open up to about the stuff that really matters.

Sometimes you might feel it's important to be popular, but it's often people who have an enormous social circle who feel the loneliest, because they aren't really close to anyone.

A FRIEND FOR EVERY MOOD

There are some friends you might share absolutely everything with, but not every friendship involves talking about feelings or sharing every detail of your life. Sometimes, you might just want to spend time with someone who makes you laugh, or who shares your hobbies. These types of friendships can make your life better, too.

THE FAMILY FRIEND

Sometimes, you need someone to help liven up family events. You might only see your cousins or the children of your parents' or carers' friends once a year, but having someone around can be a blessing in a sea of adults.

THE IN-JOKE FRIEND

Someone who gets your weird jokes
and finds you funny can give you
a glow. Sharing in-jokes makes you
feel part of a secret club.

THE HOBBY FRIEND

A friend with common
interests gives you the chance
to share your passion.

THE TEAM-MATE

Sharing the ups and downs of winning and losing creates an
important bond — even if you never see your team-mates
when they aren't in sports kit and covered in mud.

BEST FRIENDS... FOREVER?

Although you might find friends in your life that you think will be your best friends forever and ever, friendship isn't set in stone. As you grow and change, your friendships may too. You might drift apart from some of your friends when you move schools, or develop new interests. That's completely natural, and you don't have to keep the same people in your life forever.

To be honest, we stopped having anything in common about 400 years ago...

HOW TO MAKE NEW FRIENDS

When you start a new school, move house or just feel like meeting new people, it can be daunting knowing how to find friends.

- Join things: clubs, music groups, sports teams and so on. That way you're likely to meet a) more new people and b) people who share your interests and passions.
- Be open-minded: don't limit yourself to one type of person and don't make judgements before you get to know someone.
- Smile, chat, and ask questions (without being nosy) to get to know someone.
- Be patient: friendships can take a while to develop. If you don't immediately become best friends with someone, that doesn't mean you won't become close in time. Don't put pressure on yourself to become best friends with the first person you meet.

TOXIC FRIENDSHIPS

Some friendships aren't good for you.

They're sometimes called toxic friendships,

because they're an emotional version of poison.

A toxic friend might...

- Tell you you're wrong all the time, whatever you say.
- Constantly criticize things you do and remind you of embarrassing things you've done in the past.
- Make you feel bad in some way you can't put your finger on when you're together.
- Tell you who you can or can't spend time with.
- Say horrible things about other people and try to make you say horrible things about them, as well.
- Try to make you do things you don't want to do, including things that might get you into trouble.
- Talk down or belittle things you're interested in or good at.

HOW TO HANDLE TOXIC PEOPLE

You may go your whole life without coming across a toxic friend. But if you do find you're spending time with someone who's bad for you, you have a few choices.

If you feel comfortable, you could talk to them about how their behaviour makes you feel. They may or may not change, but telling them that what they're doing isn't OK will help you feel more in control either way.

If you don't feel comfortable confronting them, try to keep them at more of a distance. For example, don't tell them very personal things, and don't go out of your way to see them.

BEING YOURSELF

In a group of friends, it can be tempting to play a fixed role and just behave in the way people expect you to. For example, if you get a reputation for being the joker in the group, you might feel that you have to crack jokes all the time, even though you might feel more like sitting back and listening, or talking about something serious.

But sometimes I just want a hug...

Trying to act out one particular version of yourself all the time – or pretending to be someone you're not – is very tiring and stressful. Any friend who's a positive influence on your life won't want the fake version of you, so you can relax and allow yourself to express all the parts of your personality.

PEER PRESSURE

Friends can be a powerful influence, and trying to please or impress them can sometimes land you in trouble.

Friends making you do stuff you wouldn't normally do is called peer pressure – it might be encouraging you to cause trouble in school, pushing you to try something you shouldn't, or even persuading you to do something illegal.

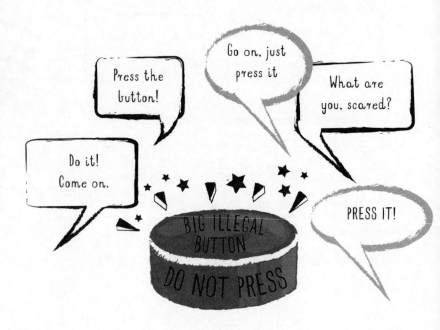

Peer pressure can feel like an inevitable part of friendships – a rite of passage you have to go through, but it's not. You can always say "No". You know whether something is right or wrong, and, as you get older, you need to start taking responsibility, and thinking about the consequences of the things you do. In the worst cases, peer pressure could put you in danger, or get you into serious trouble. What might feel funny at the time, when you're joking together and egging someone on, might not feel that funny when the police or an ambulance turns up.

It doesn't always feel easy to say no to your friends – you might worry they'll make fun of you, leave you out, or laugh at you if you don't do something. Being confident in yourself can help you make sensible choices. A good friend should respect your decision and what you want to do.

UPS AND DOWNS

Even the strongest friendships have ups and downs. Arguments or awkward moments are just part of the natural rhythm of things – it doesn't mean a friendship is over. There are lots of ways to improve your friendships and solve problems by talking them over, or changing how you act.

- Think about the situation from the other person's point of view. If they're upset, is there something you've done wrong? Is there something you could avoid doing in future?
- Don't expect your friends to be psychic. If you're upset about something, tell them.
- Be willing to compromise and not get what you want all the time. For example, if the two of you always end up going to see the movie YOU want to see, or

going to the place you want to go, decide to let the other person choose every other time.

- Be assertive: you're allowed to ask for what you want and say when you're not comfortable. For example, if a friend is asking you to do something that scares you, or you think is wrong, you're not being a bad friend by saying "No".

SUPPORTING FRIENDS

You might find that friends come to talk to you about problems they're having, especially if you're a good listener and offer good advice. That's a wonderful thing, but it might mean that you end up taking on a lot of people's worries.

That can be quite a burden for you to bear. It's important to take time to look after your own worries as well as other people's. It's never your responsibility to fix anyone's problems or make them better.

BULLYING

Everyone can be mean sometimes. But when meanness and cruelty happen over a long period of time and are focused on a particular person, it is bullying. Bullying isn't always easy to spot. There are some obvious forms of bullying, such as beating someone up, threatening to hurt them, or calling them horrible names. But there are some more subtle forms too.

Bullying can also mean...
- Excluding someone on purpose.
- Spreading lies and rumours.
- Mimicking someone in a mocking voice.
- Making negative facial expressions when someone speaks, such as eye-rolling, or responding negatively to everything they suggest.
- Tripping people up, pushing them, or not letting them go past in the corridor. Physical

bullying doesn't have to mean
punching someone.

- Online bullying or sending mean emails or
messages. This is called cyberbullying.
There's more about it in Chapter 9.

THE EFFECTS OF BULLYING

Being bullied can have a very bad
effect on someone's mental health.
A bullied person might:

- Find it hard to concentrate.
- Feel sad even when the bullying stops.
- Lose their appetite or eat for comfort.
- Withdraw and not want to spend time
with other people.
- Find it hard to sleep.

WHY ME?

If you ever get bullied, you might find yourself wondering why the bully (or bullies) are picking on you.

Some victims of bullying start to blame themselves. However, it is always the bully's fault. Some people are bullied about their looks, their sexuality (see page 130), their race, their religion, how clever they are, where they live, how much money they have... but it's never really because of those things. It's about the bully.

Your mum's foreign, isn't she? I bet she eats frogs.*

*Translation: I'm a racist who has no knowledge of other cultures and am desperately trying to hide my own fear and ignorance.

Some people bully because they feel insecure or envious, or don't know how to express their emotions. Other bullies just enjoy being cruel.

COPING WITH BULLYING

Sharing what you're going through with an adult you trust is a good first step. They can help you take practical steps to make things better. If the bullying is happening at school, you could talk to your school counsellor – they will have lots of advice to help you deal with bullies and stay safe and happy at school. Schools usually also have someone trained in young people's mental health, who will be able to provide support to help you feel better, if it's getting you down or making you anxious.

If you feel nervous or self-conscious going to talk to an adult at school, you could write them a note explaining what's happening, and that you're not sure how to bring it up. They will be able to work with you discreetly to sort things out.

You don't have to mention it at school to start with. You could try talking to your parent or carer at home, or a more distant member of your family. Once you let someone know, they can work with you to try to fix it.

AM I A BULLY?

If you think you might be bullying someone, it's not too late to stop. Think very hard about the effect your actions might be having. Talk to someone at home or a teacher at school. You might bully someone because you're actually not very happy yourself, in which case, they should be able to offer you support or help you feel better.

SPENDING TIME ALONE

Everyone needs some time
away from other people.
There won't always be people
around you, and when there

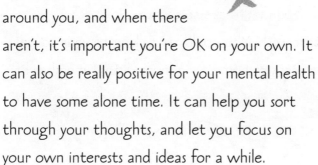

aren't, it's important you're OK on your own. It
can also be really positive for your mental health
to have some alone time. It can help you sort
through your thoughts, and let you focus on
your own interests and ideas for a while.

Enjoying your own company doesn't come
naturally to everyone. Some people feel anxious
when they're alone and not sure what to do
with their thoughts. Learning to be alone can
take time.

If being on your own feels unnatural, here
are some things to try:

• Sit quietly or go for a walk and allow your
   mind to wander. You might find interesting
   thoughts surface, that might not pop up

while you're around other people.

- Listen to music that moves you and sit
  (or lie) there in a puddle of feelings.
  Take time to feel the emotions, rather
  than pushing them away.

- Scribble or doodle on a pad, without trying
  to draw anything in particular. Just let your
  hand take the line wherever it wants to go.

Sometimes, when you're having friendship worries, doing something for other people can help you feel better.

Being reminded that other people struggle and face difficulties won't cure your problems...

> You should be *grateful* for having exams. Some children don't get to have an education at all.

...but knowing that you have the power to do something to help them can build your confidence and your sense of self-worth. You could try:

Raising money to give to charity with your friends.

Making time to chat and listen to a friend having a hard time.

Helping a sibling or friend with their homework.

7. FAMILY

EVERY FAMILY IS DIFFERENT

Your family has a big impact on your mental health, not just now, but for your whole life. You've probably noticed from talking to friends or going to their homes that their families look different or work in a different way to yours. Every family is different, both in terms of the people who are part of it, and the way those people live and interact.

Most of the time, your family should have a positive effect on your mental health, through teaching you stuff, loving you, supporting you, and trying to get you to grow up into the best adult you can be. But that's not the case for everyone, and even if it is, it doesn't always feel like that. As you grow up it's normal to find life at home quite difficult at times.

This chapter is about how to keep a good relationship with family, and how to deal with any bigger, more difficult complications your family has to go through.

The things in this chapter might be happening to you, or might happen in the future, but they might not. They're not certain or inevitable, but it's good for you to know about them so you know what to expect if they happen to you, and so you can show understanding to other people who are going through them.

YOUR FAMILY MIGHT HAVE...

No children

FOSTERED CHILDREN

LOTS OF CHILDREN

ADOPTED CHILDREN

TWO DADS

ONE PARENT OR CARER

TWO PARENTS OR CARERS

STEP-PARENTS

STEP-SIBLINGS

Two mums

HALF-SIBLINGS

A BIG HOUSE AND A BIG GARDEN

A SMALL HOUSE OR FLAT WITHOUT MUCH SPARE SPACE

SOMEONE WITH A DISABILITY

SOMEONE WHO DIED AND ISN'T AROUND ANY MORE

SOMEONE WHO'S ILL, AND NEEDS LOOKING AFTER

PEOPLE LIVING IN DIFFERENT COUNTRIES

THE WHOLE EXTENDED FAMILY LIVING UNDER ONE ROOF

PEOPLE WITH DIFFERENT RELIGIOUS BELIEFS

LOTS OF PETS

SOMEONE IN THE MILITARY

People who are best friends

PEOPLE WHO DON'T GET ON

People who speak different languages

LOADS OF MONEY

PROBLEMS WITH MONEY

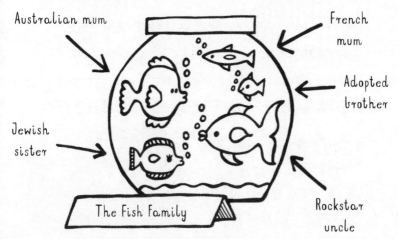

Australian mum

French mum

Adopted brother

Jewish sister

Rockstar uncle

The Fish Family

ANGER

For a lot of young people (and adults too), a common problem in families is feeling angry – family members often annoy each other, or get cross and lash out. You might feel you can get away with saying things in angry outbursts at home that you wouldn't dare say to a friend or someone at school, because your family will forgive you and keep on loving you. Even if that's true, lots of angry shouting matches, door-slamming or stubborn silences are not good for anyone's mental health, and there are usually healthier ways to deal with things.

Anger isn't always a negative emotion. It can be useful for working out what you think the 'right' thing is, and for building ideas and opinions. You can feel angry, but shouldn't hurt or bully anyone in your family because of it. For more about the science of anger look back to page 27.

As you go through puberty, the increased levels of hormones flying around your body can make you more likely to feel strong emotions. Lots of different feelings can end up coming out as anger – that's normal, and it's part of the big changes you're going through as a teenager.

CALMING DOWN

Feeling angry a lot can wind you up, making it hard for you to concentrate at school, relax, and sleep. If you find yourself getting very angry, before exploding, try:

* Taking several deep breaths in and out. Let the hot anger seep away, if you can, making time to feel calmer and more rational about the argument.

3

2

1

Count to three
as you breathe
in slowly...

1

2

3

...then count
to three as you
breathe out slowly.

* Find a piece of music or audiobook that you find soothing and listen to it when you feel cross. It could be piano music or a film soundtrack, or a book from your childhood.

- If a discussion is getting heated, think about it from the other person's point of view, and see if you can reach an agreement calmly. You're still allowed to put your point across, but you're more likely to come to a conclusion together in a conversation than in an argument.
- Write down in a notebook what you're angry about. Come back to it later when you've relaxed, and see how you feel about it then.

Sometimes when you calm down, you realize that there was a different feeling underneath the anger — maybe you felt scared, or threatened, or simply hungry or tired. Finding a feeling underneath anger, if there is one, can help you work out how to feel better.

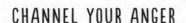

CHANNEL YOUR ANGER

You could try channelling your anger and turning it into something productive by doing one of these:

- Go for a walk or a short run. Getting fresh air and a little light exercise can help you let off some steam and give you time to process your thoughts.

- Sing loudly or dance vigorously — get the blood pumping, open those windpipes and shake it off (maybe just go for the dancing with headphones option if there are people in the house trying to sleep or watch TV...).

- Start a long-term project, such as writing a diary to express all those feelings, or a craft creation that you can come back to each time you feel your temper rising. Concentrating will take your mind off whatever is making you angry and creating something will give you a sense of achievement.

- Build bridges. If you've been arguing with a sibling, take time to chat or play instead. If you were angry with a parent or carer, you could offer to help with dinner. Build up the respect between you and get on the same side. It'll benefit both of you in the long run.

- If your anger stems from something you think is unjust, from a political issue such as homophobia, social welfare, or climate change, you could use your anger to do something about it. Write to a local politician, research it online, or raise awareness by talking to your friends about it.

Dear Prime Minister,

INDEPENDENCE

As you get older, it's natural to want to be more independent – to do things without all your family around, take more responsibility and go places alone or with friends. This can become a sticking point with your family, especaially if you feel ready to go out and do things on your own before they are ready to let you. You might feel belittled, or undermined if someone says you can't go out to the park, shops, or cinema on your own, and this can affect your self-esteem.

Remember it's a parent or carer's job to keep you safe, and they might be cautious about giving you lots of independence. Parents and carers set boundaries that they are comfortable with, and those boundaries may not be the same as those of your friends. Just because someone you know is allowed to go to a certain party doesn't mean your parents or carers have to let you go too.

At the end of the day, parents will use their common sense to try to make sure you're safe. Trust their judgement – they've been around for a lot longer than you and know what's a good idea and what's not. You might need to work together to come to agreements, and you'll probably need to prove you're responsible enough to take more independence.

To earn more independence, you could try:
- Offering to pop to the supermarket, to get any supplies that are needed.
- Agreeing to walk or travel to school by yourself, or with friends on set days.
- Do more jobs around the house, to prove you take your responsibility seriously.
- Take on a leadership role at school or in a club, like being the captain of a team, a prefect, or a buddy or mentor for someone younger.

DIVORCE AND SEPARATION

Sometimes, it's not just your anger or conflict you have to deal with. In many families, parents' or carers' anger, annoyance or frustration at each other can lead to them deciding not to be together any more. This process is called separation or divorce, and it happens to about 40% of married couples in the UK and Europe.

If your parents or carers split up, it can have a big effect on you. It might mean a lot of changes to get used to, and probably some difficult feelings and emotions to deal with.

WHY DO PEOPLE SPLIT UP?

Relationships don't always stay as happy and easy as they were to start with. Over time, everyone changes slightly, and what they want, love, and think about other people can change too.

Occasionally, someone in the relationship can become violent, or dependent on drugs or alcohol, which can make life difficult, and even frightening.

Whatever the reasons, a couple choosing to separate think that for the sake of the safety and mental health of themselves and their families, they should split up. Though it can be a challenge, separation is often the best thing for a family in the long run.

WHAT HAPPENS?

All separations are slightly different, but a lot involve some kind of legal process to divide up belongings, money and time with children. Divorce is a specific type of separation that officially ends a couple's marriage.

LEGAL STUFF

CHANGES

Almost always, when a couple splits up, there are changes. Those changes might include:

- Moving house.
- Going to a new school if you move to a new area.
- Spending some time with each parent, which might mean living in two different places.
- Seeing one parent less than the other one.
- Having new members of your family, such as step-parents, step-siblings or half-siblings.
- Dealing with parents who don't seem to like each other any more.
- Not doing the things you used to do together as a family, for example going on holiday.

It can take time to get used to these changes, and you might feel unsettled for a while.

If your parents do separate, and you are finding it hard, there are many people you can talk to. You might not want to talk to your parents themselves, as they may seem stressed, distracted or upset. That's OK. You could talk to other members of your family, who are going through it too, such as siblings, or grandparents, or you could talk to a teacher or counsellor about it at school. If you'd prefer not to talk about it, you don't have to.

Whatever happens and however you feel, remember things were NOT your fault. Things will settle down over time – after a while, even big changes start to feel normal.

BEREAVEMENT

One of the hardest things for a family to deal with is the death of a loved one.

If someone close to you does die, it can help to:

- Allow yourself to feel upset. Pressing down and stopping sadness doesn't really help in the long run.
- Take time to understand and digest what has happened. Don't expect to feel better about it quickly. Over time it will hurt less.
- Talk about the person who died, or look at pictures and remember funny stories about them.

Grandpa's photos

It can be particularly sad or scary to see your parents or carers upset. Try to remember that it's not your responsibility to make them feel better – they're allowed to be sad for a while, just like you are. Talking together, making sure you eat, sleep, and get fresh air, and trying to stay calm and relaxed might help a little.

There's no right or wrong way to feel when someone dies. It's OK if you don't feel that sad, or if you don't really understand what's going on. It's also OK if you're really, really upset or if you feel very angry. Everyone feels a little different when someone dies, and everyone deals with it differently.

DISABILITY

Living with a disability, or supporting someone else with a disability, can affect your mental health.

'Disability' is a really broad term, covering all kinds of conditions that affect or impair how someone lives, moves, acts, and experiences the world. Disabilities can affect someone's body, brain or senses, or a combination of all three.

It doesn't always, but living with a disability can present extra challenges, and it can dent your confidence and self-esteem. Supporting someone in your family with a disability can also be challenging, and impact the way you live.

It's OK if you feel down about it sometimes, whether the disability is yours, or someone else's. It's also OK never to feel down about it at all.

Every disability is different. Some have very little effect on someone's life, while some dictate everything that person does. Some disabilities are there from birth, and others occur or develop during someone's life.

It's easy to tell someone has a disability if they use a wheelchair or have a guide dog to help them get around, but a lot of disabilities, such as mental health conditions and learning difficulties, can be hard to spot.

Nobody should ever be bullied, disadvantaged, or treated badly because of a disability.

THE LAW

In most countries, it is illegal to discriminate against someone with a disability — for example in school admission or employment processes.

Here are some examples of conditions covered in the umbrella term of 'disability':

Severe asthma
Autism
Diabetes
DEAFNESS
DEPRESSION
Dyslexia
BLINDNESS
ADHD
(ATTENTION DEFICIT
HYPERACTIVITY DISORDER)
Asperger syndrome
Epilepsy
Crohn's disease
CEREBRAL PALSY
Arthritis
MS
(MULTIPLE SCLEROSIS)

WHAT TO DO

If you have a disability yourself, you might find it never negatively impacts upon your life. But there's a chance it might make some things more difficult for you, and you might find it affects your confidence or makes you feel left out.

No one should ever make you feel inferior, miserable, or victimized because of your disability. If you think someone is bullying you, tell an adult you trust, such as a teacher or a family member.

If one of your friends or family has a disability, they might find certain things you want to do quite difficult. Bear them in mind, and make sure that plans suit everyone.

For links to websites with advice on living with a disability, go to the Usborne Quicklinks website (see page 256).

SEX AND ROMANCE

DIFFERENT FEELINGS

As you grow up and go through puberty, you might start to have feelings for other people – romantic feelings that are different to feelings you've had before. That might be exciting, it might fill you with dread, or it might just make you cringe.

However you feel about it, entering the world of relationships can be daunting, and worrying can have an impact on your mental health. It can make you feel uncertain, and you might compare yourself to other people more than you have before. Trying to work out who you are and who you might like isn't always easy, but having good, positive mental health can help you navigate through everything.

You may not fancy anyone at the moment or want to date at all, but as a teenager you'll probably hear other people start to talk about it.

125

FANCY THAT

You might hear a lot of people
talking about who they 'fancy', or
have a 'crush on'. Having a crush on
someone is common, and sometimes pleasant,
but it can be a little confusing.

You might have a crush on someone you
know, but it's also common to have crushes on
people you don't know – particularly celebrities.
Crushes normally fade away after a few weeks.

Starting to fancy people means you can work
out what you like in other people, what qualities
you admire, and what you find attractive. It
could be being good at sports, being smart, being
funny, or something you can't even explain –
everyone finds different things attractive.

How do you know if you have a crush on someone?

- Do you really like them, and admire things about them?
- Do you get nervous when you see them and struggle to get your words out properly, or say strange things by accident?

- Do you get a fluttery feeling in your stomach when you see them?

IT'S OK IF...

YOU DON'T
WANT A
RELATIONSHIP

YOU DO WANT A
RELATIONSHIP

YOU FEEL LIKE YOU'RE
THE ONLY PERSON NOT
IN A RELATIONSHIP

YOU LIKE
GIRLS

YOU LIKE BOYS

YOU LIKE EVERYONE

YOU LIKE
NO ONE

YOU CHANGE YOUR MIND

YOU START DATING
WHEN YOU'RE A
PENSIONER

YOU START DATING
WHEN YOU'RE A
TEENAGER

You date one
person all your life

YOU DATE
ONE HUNDRED
PEOPLE

YOU NEVER
DATE ANYONE

You fall in love

YOU DON'T
FALL IN LOVE

SOMEONE FALLS IN LOVE
WITH YOU BUT YOU DON'T
LOVE THEM BACK

GIVE IT A NAME

The group of people that someone is attracted to determines what is known as their sexuality. You don't have to be sure of your sexuality now, or ever, but it's important to be aware that not everyone feels the same. There is no way of being or feeling that is better, worse or more 'normal' than any other.

It's up to you to figure out what you like and decide what you want to call it, or if you want to call it anything at all. No one else should decide for you, or tell you how you feel. Your sexuality is something that you may already know, or it might take years more to find out.

Some people find it useful and important to give their sexuality a name. Some people don't. Here are some of the words people use to describe different sexualities:

- **HETEROSEXUAL** – fancy people of a different gender. Some people call this being 'straight'.

- **HOMOSEXUAL** – fancy people of the same gender. This is usually known as being 'gay'. Gay girls are often called lesbians.

- **BISEXUAL** – fancy people of more than one gender. Bisexual people may fancy one gender more than the other, or both equally.

- **ASEXUAL** – not physically attracted to anyone. At the moment you may not feel attracted to anyone, but that doesn't necessarily mean you're asexual. As you grow older it might become clearer - be patient and give yourself time to see what you think.

- **PANSEXUAL** - fancy people of all genders.

Sexualities are on a scale, also called a spectrum, and the boundaries between different sexualities can be loose. For example you might be a heterosexual girl, and only ever fancy boys, or you might be a heterosexual girl who fancies girls sometimes too.

For more terms associated with gender and sexuality, go to the glossary on page 257. For links to websites with more information about sexualities, visit the Usborne Quicklinks website (see page 256).

COMING OUT

Often, people assume that everyone is straight, unless they are told otherwise. When someone chooses to tell other people that they're not heterosexual, it is known as 'coming out'.

Coming out can be nerve-wracking and stressful – some people are scared to tell others for fear of how they'll react. Others find it natural and easy, and some may feel they don't need to come out at all.

Coming out can also be about saying "I'm ready to talk about this with you", not just about letting other people know.

I've got news! I'm a lesbian!

Yes, but what's the news?

If someone talks to you about their sexuality, listen and be supportive.

For many people, coming out is a positive experience, and others are supportive and loving. But for some people this isn't the case. In some families, cultures and situations where sexualities other than heterosexuality aren't widely accepted, coming out can be harder.

If someone reacts badly to the news, makes fun of you, or starts bullying you, it is because they are ignorant and need to develop more understanding. They might also be uncomfortable or stuggling to understand their own sexuality. However hard it is, try to bear in mind that it is their lack of understanding rather than anything about you that has made them react like that.

You might think coming out will change how people think of you, and how people treat you. It shouldn't – you are still you, and nothing has really changed. You don't suddenly start living a 'gay' life, it's just the same as before.

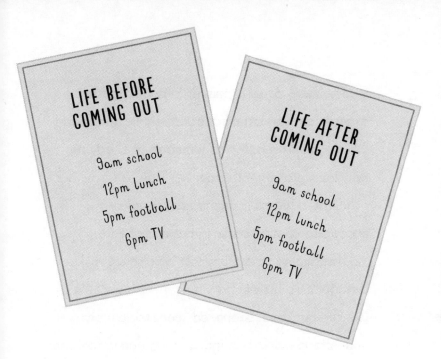

LIFE BEFORE COMING OUT

9am school
12pm lunch
5pm football
6pm TV

LIFE AFTER COMING OUT

9am school
12pm lunch
5pm football
6pm TV

THE UGLY TRUTH

Unfortunately not everyone is supportive of other people's sexualities. Some people don't believe a relationship should exist with anyone other than someone of the opposite sex. This is known as homophobia – being scared of non-heterosexual relationships.

In over 20 countries around the world, including England, Wales, Scotland, the USA, and most of Europe, gay and straight people have equal rights. But it's not the same everywhere. In some countries it's illegal even to have a relationship with someone of the same sex, let alone get married.

Despite equal rights in many countries, some people still feel a stigma attached to homosexuality, and many still experience homophobic bullying.

Even if other people do seem to, try not to use words like 'gay' in an offhand, negative way (for example "that's so gay"). Homophobic bullying is not acceptable under any circumstances, and if you see any, or are being bullied yourself, tell a teacher or adult you trust.

GOOD RELATIONSHIPS

Romantic relationships come in many forms. Some are very casual and relaxed, some are intense and full of emotions.

There's no right way to have a relationship, as long as it's equal and enjoyable. A good relationship is always based on respect.

BAD RELATIONSHIPS

Not all relationships are good. A range of things can make a relationship bad – negative feelings such as anxiety and jealousy can take the enjoyment away from a relationship.

If you ever find yourself in a relationship where someone treats you badly, hurts you, controls you, or puts pressure on you to do things you don't want to do, it's a bad relationship. In that case, for the sake of your physical and mental health, you should end it. Even if you think you're in love, and still like some things about that person, the fact they do not treat you as an equal is dangerous.

BREAK-UPS

Even good relationships don't always last forever. Break-ups can be difficult, however they happen. You'll probably have got used to seeing the other person a lot, and will miss having them around. If you didn't want it to end, you might feel you weren't good enough for the other person and might feel negative about yourself. You're allowed to feel sad for a while – it's healthier to think about and process your emotions than bottle them up and hold them all in.

If you are breaking up with someone, do it in person, face-to-face. Be honest, but gentle, and try not to hurt their feelings.

SEX

During puberty, your sexual organs develop. The chemicals in your body called hormones also change a lot. These combine to prepare you for a sexual relationship. Not everyone develops at the same rate, but it's likely that during your teenage years you'll be physically equipped for the sex part of an adult relationship. But being physically ready does not necessarily mean you're emotionally ready, and working out how you feel about it can be a scary part of growing up.

It can be stressful thinking you don't know much, and everyone else seems to, so here are some common questions and answers about sex.

1. IS EVERYONE ELSE HAVING SEX?

As you grow up people will probably talk about sex more and more. It may sound like everybody is doing it, and you might feel pressure to catch up. Actually, it's probably just all talk – the average age that people first have sex is about 17, but many people do it when they're older, and that's perfectly normal.

2. IS IT OK IF I DON'T WANT TO HAVE SEX?

Absolutely! Most people don't feel they want to until they're well into puberty, and you legally need be at least 16 before you have sex anyway.

Don't think you're weird if you're not at all interested right now – that's natural and normal. There's not an age when you suddenly have to start having sex either. No one else can decide if and when you want to and are ready – that's up to you.

3. WHO CAN HAVE SEX?

People believe different things about who should have sex and when they should have it, but in the eyes of the law, in the UK and USA anyone can have sex, whether or not they're married, as long as they're old enough and both consent to it.

THE LAW

Sex is only legal between people over the 'age of consent'. In the UK and most of Europe, the age of consent is 16, in the USA it is between 16 and 18 depending on the state you live in. Around the world, it varies from 14 to 18, but whatever it is, it's a criminal offence for anyone under that age to have sex.

4. DO I HAVE TO HAVE SEX IF SOMEONE ELSE WANTS TO, EVEN IF I DON'T?

No. That is illegal, whatever age you are. It is only up to YOU when you have sex. (See the box on page 144.)

5. HOW DO YOU SAY NO TO SEX?

You can say no out loud, explain that you are not comfortable, and if you need to, put your hand out to show you want to stop, or even walk away. Whoever you're with should respect your decision.

YOUR BODY, YOUR RULES

As you grow up, you might want to have a physical relationship with someone. The crucial rule is you should never do anything you do not feel comfortable with. No one should push you into anything that you don't want to do. The person you're going out with should not force you to have sex, and you should not force anyone to have sex with you, if they don't want it. That is illegal and taken extremely seriously by the police.

You must always give, and have, CONSENT – that's permission. You don't need to provide a written permission slip, like for going on a school trip, but before you have sex you both need to be sure that you're OK with what's about to happen. You can also withdraw consent whilst having sex, if you become uncomfortable or scared. Saying nothing doesn't count as consent – you can't take silence for a yes.

THE LAW

Having sex with someone who has not consented is called assault, or rape, and is a very serious crime. If you ever think you have been raped, assaulted, or touched without your permission, tell an adult you trust, and contact the police if you feel able to.

AM I READY?

Contemplating sex – whether to have it, when to have it, who to have it with – can be stressful, and confusing. Try not to feel pressurized – everyone goes at their own pace during puberty, as everyone develops physically and emotionally at different rates. There's plenty of time in your life and you don't need to rush into anything as a teenager.

THERE'S MORE TO LIFE

You don't have to have sex to have a good relationship. Here are some other things you can do instead of having sex:

CHAT

INVENT SOMETHING

Hold hands

TAKE SELFIES WITH RIDICULOUS FILTERS

WATCH A FILM

PLAY BOARD GAMES

HUG AND CUDDLE

GO TO THE ZOO

Plan world domination

DO SPORTS

kiss

WRITE A POLITICAL MANIFESTO TOGETHER FIXING ALL THE COUNTRY'S PROBLEMS

Our Manifesto

SEX ON THE INTERNET

The internet is full of great things that can do wonders for your mental health. But it's also got some stuff on it that can be quite damaging, particularly when it comes to sex.

A lot of young people are exposed to sex in films, TV and online, before real life. That can cause some problems. There is a lot of sex on the internet, and though there are filters and walls that websites, companies and your parents or carers might put up, unfortunately some of it sometimes gets through.

SEX SEX SEX SEX
SEX SEX
SEX

Images and videos online of people having sex or doing sexual things is known as pornography, or 'porn' for short. In some places, porn is illegal. In others it's illegal for under 18s. Those laws exist for very good reasons. Though porn gives some people pleasure, it can create problems.

If you watch porn before you've ever had sex, you might get very unrealistic views of what naked people look like, or what sex is really like. Porn is created as a type of entertainment. It is exaggerated, fake, choreographed, and over the top. The people in it are paid to look good – they may spend huge amounts of money on their bodies, enhancing them with plastic surgery or expensive treatments. In real life, people don't all look like that, and no one should expect you to look like that (look back to Chapter 5 for more on body image).

If anyone ever tries to show you images or videos that you don't want to see, say no, and walk away. You do not have to look at anything you don't want to.

HELPFUL NOTE: Not all naked pictures online are pornographic – some of them are scientific diagrams, some are Ancient Greek statues, some are painted portraits. You're allowed to see those pictures, so don't worry if you stumble across one while doing your homework. Pornography is specifically designed to sexually arouse people.

Some people in relationships send naked photos to each other online or by text. This is known as sexting. Remember, even if you really trust the person you're sending the photos to, someone else could get hold of them, and things can spread very fast online. That can make you feel vulnerable, upset, and insecure. If anyone ever sends you a naked photo, never send it on to anyone else. If the person in the photo is under 18, you could be breaking the law.

THE LAW

It is illegal to possess or distribute naked or sexual photos of children, even if you're a child yourself. It is a very serious crime, and could turn a joke with your friends into a criminal record.

STOP — THINK BEFORE YOU SEND.

ON THE INTERNET

THE GOOD...

The internet is an amazing thing – for finding out information, connecting with the rest of the world, and watching videos of animals sneezing. If you use it carefully, it can be a really positive resource, and something you'll probably need almost every day throughout your life.

THE BAD...

Unfortunately the internet isn't amazing all the time. Spending a lot of time on social media, and comparing your life to the lives you see portrayed on there, can have a negative impact on your mental health, especially while you're growing up. This chapter will go through some of the risks associated with life online, particularly social media, and give you tips on how to use the internet sensibly and healthily, and how to get the most out of it.

...AND THE UGLY

The internet also contains some seriously bad things – from dangerous, to illegal. Though you don't have to be worried about them, and you may never come across them, it's worth being aware of them to help protect yourself.

Whether you use a phone, tablet or computer to go online, it's good to know how to use the internet in a way that has a positive effect on your mental health.

SOCIAL MEDIA

Today, a large proportion of internet activity
is on social media. Social media sites and apps
help you connect with friends, family and even
celebrities, which can be great. But creating
and maintaining a life online can be hard
work too.

LIKES

When you post a picture, opinion or idea on
social media, other people can 'like' it. That
means if people *don't* 'like' it, it can feel quite
painful, and the need to get a certain number of
likes or comments can end up being stressful.

Only 20,127
'likes'. Better
delete it.

For a lot of people, self-esteem and confidence is tied up with numbers of 'likes'. More likes = more confidence. The trouble with that is not getting enough 'likes' can dent your self-esteem, and that can have a negative impact on your mental health. Though it's easy to get caught up in it all, remember that 'likes' don't actually mean very much – they don't give you more love, more worth or more value. You are not dependent on how many 'likes' you get, and you're more than the photos you post online.

TRY THIS

Write down or think about three things you really like about one of your friends. Then write down three things you think they like about you (if you're not sure or can't think of any, ask them!)

Those things you write down are bigger and more important than any 'likes' you give out or receive on social media.

THE SCIENCE OF LIKES

You're allowed to want 'likes' - it's completely natural. In fact, getting a 'like' online triggers the same reward pathway in the brain as getting food, money or praise. So science says we're wired to like 'likes'. But the reward pathway has a downside too - we can get addicted to the good feeling, and want it again and again, more and more. Scientists think lots of people, especially teenagers, are addicted to getting 'likes' online, and so feel bad when they don't get enough.

It can also be stressful trying to keep up with everyone else's posts. It often leads to spending a lot of time on social media, just scrolling and liking endlessly. If it's getting too much, step away from it.

SNAPSHOT LIVES

The photos and videos you see on people's social media accounts are just selected snapshots of their lives – the best outfits, views, meals, their best hair days...

What you don't see is the other 90% of their life – the arguments, the sniffly colds, the cranky days, the little failures. For every happy photo you see, there were probably lots of unhappy moments – you are not the only one who feels sad, bad, ugly or a bit of a failure sometimes.

Even celebrities whose accounts you might follow, for all their money, fame and support, will have those down days, or weeks. Comparing yourself to the people you *think* you see online will probably make you feel miserable. People might be looking at the pictures you post and thinking the same.

The finished photo you see may not be
telling the whole story.

Is actually
feeling really
sad and
worried.

Only put these clothes
on for the photo

Spent an hour on hair
and make-up before
taking selfie.

Has a horrible cold and
is using a lot of filters
to not look ill.

It's OK to use social media, and to put up those snapshot photos, but remember to fill in the gaps between the photos in your head – no one's life is perfect, however beautiful, together and ideal their online life looks.

What you see

What you don't see

YOUR ONLINE PERSONA

Chapter 4 was about working out your identity, and how you present yourself to other people in your life. The same happens online – you have an online personality that you are presenting to people you know and don't know on the internet. You are in control of what other people see, and bit by bit, across all the sites you post or message on, you build up an online personality that has a reputation, just like you do in real life.

You might have an online personality almost identical to your real-life personality, but a lot of people have an online alter-ego; a more exaggerated, extreme or confident version of themselves. Some people even pretend to be someone else entirely. In a way that's a good thing about social media, because it can give people more confidence than they might have face-to-face, especially in the difficult, often awkward times of puberty. But there are negative sides to it too. As well as the snapshot problem, you, or others, might say or do things online you wouldn't do in real life – such as be mean, say rude things, or send sexual photos or messages that you wouldn't share in person.

OVERSHARING

Stuff sticks around on the internet. Even if you try to delete it, once something is posted or sent, it can't be erased completely. So if you say something nasty to someone, or post or send something you might regret, there's always a trace of it somewhere.

CYBERBULLYING

It's easy to say nasty things online, when you're just typing words into a little box. But behind that little box is a real person, just like you, on a phone or on a computer. Saying horrible things online is known as cyberbullying, and it can really damage people's mental health (just like bullying people face-to-face).

Though it can't be physically violent, cyberbullying can be worse than face-to-face bullying because there's no escaping from it.

You don't leave it at the school gate, and can't walk away - cyberbullies can be there wherever there is an internet connection.

Cyberbully

Cyberbullying includes:

- Sending cruel, nasty or humiliating messages, either privately or on public pages
- Forwarding embarrassing videos or photos on to people
- Giving out someone's personal details such as their address or phone number, without their permission. This is sometimes known as doxxing.
- Sending unwanted sexual messages or images to people
- Making abusive comments about someone – including homophobic, racist, transphobic or sexist comments

There are other ways to cyberbully someone as well – if anyone does or says anything to you online that makes you uncomfortable, or hurts your feelings, then you should take action.

Sometimes people are trying to be funny, but unfortunately joking online often comes across as rudeness. If it's a one-time thing, you could try to ignore it, or talk to the person about it, or maybe just point out the joke didn't really work. For anything more serious, or anything that happens more than once, tell an adult you trust. If it involves people at school, let a teacher or school counsellor know.

Keep your eyes out on social media for other people being cyberbullied too. You probably wouldn't watch someone get beaten up and walk away without telling anyone, so the same applies online. You don't have to wade into the argument online and get caught in the middle of it, but by noticing and informing someone you could really help the person getting bullied. Remember though – it is NOT your responsibility to stop or fix cyberbullying. If it's happening to you or anyone else...

...IT IS NOT YOUR FAULT.

Everyone deserves to be able to use the internet and all its great websites without being intimidated, harassed or humiliated.

TRIGGER WARNINGS

Social media helps a lot of people with mental health problems, who find an online community to share their struggles and victories with. When people post about things that someone else might find hard to read or see, or that might cause someone else to feel bad, they usually put the words 'Trigger Warning' near the start of the post.

If you see a post that says Trigger Warning, or TW on it, the content might be upsetting.

For lots more about mental health problems, and advice about dealing with them, go to Chapter 11.

TAKE A BREAK

Some big scientific studies in America have shown that there's a correlation between how long someone's on social media, and how likely they are to have a mental health problem such as depression. (That doesn't mean social media *causes* them, they can just be linked). It's OK to use social media, but, for the good of your mental health, it is a very good idea to take a break sometimes.

You could:

- Choose one evening each week where you don't look at any social media sites.
- Pick a weekend and leave your phone off completely (or use it just to make necessary calls).
- Ignore social media when you go on holiday. Enjoy the time with your family or friends instead.
- As well as having some time in the week completely away from social media, it might be a good idea to *cut down* the amount of time you do spend on it. For example, if you normally spend two hours a day on it, try reducing that to one hour.

MORE TO LIFE

Stuff you can do in your spare time other than go on social media:

READ A BOOK

PLAY A
BOARD
GAME

Relax in
the bath

GO FOR A
WALK, SWIM
OR CYCLE RIDE

KEEP A DIARY

DIARIES ARE GOOD WAYS OF
PROCESSING WHAT YOU'RE
THINKING AND HOW THINGS ARE
GOING SO THIS IS A POSITIVE THING
TO DO FOR YOUR MENTAL HEALTH.

MAKE UP A
DANCE

WORK
ON YOUR
KEEPY-UPPY
SKILLS.

LISTEN TO MUSIC,
OR AN AUDIOBOOK

WRITE THAT
GREAT STORY
YOU'VE BEEN
THINKING ABOUT

TAKE
PHOTOS

Cook or bake something

SING

LEARN TO
JUGGLE –
A GOOD
LIFE SKILL

DO
YOUR
HOMEWORK

Try sketching
or painting

GENERAL ONLINE SAFETY

As well as all the other things in this chapter,
keep yourself safe by:

- Never posting your address or phone number online.
- Don't meet anyone you've talked to online if you
  don't know who they are. If you do meet someone
  you've met online, even if you think you know them,
  tell other people when and where you are going, and
  go with a trusted adult to start with.
- Don't send or share naked photos of anyone – if they
  are under 18 this is against the law, and is a very
  serious crime. That includes pictures of yourself.
- Don't look at or watch anything you're not
  comfortable with.
- Don't type anyone's bankcard details anywhere
  without the owner's permission.

DIFFICULT TIMES

10

SOMETIMES LIFE IS HARD

Unfortunately there are lots of difficult things in life that almost all of us will face at some point. These difficult things tend to come and go – they might be hard for a little while but they don't last forever. This chapter will go through some of the difficulties you're likely to face, and give you some tips to help you deal with them.

CHALLENGES AT SCHOOL

The likelihood is, unless you are taught at home, you spend a lot of your life at school. That's great in many ways: it's where you learn things, prepare for a job and adult life, take part in clubs and hobbies, and it's probably where you've got friends too. But school life isn't always easy.

PRESSURE

As you get older and go to secondary or high school, you'll probably start to feel pressure. People will be telling you that what you do now counts, affects your future, and can influence the job you get as an adult. Your teachers and family may start to worry more about the grades you're getting, and how hard you're working.

Those things can add up to make you feel under a lot of pressure, and that pressure can build up over the years in school and make you feel stressed and sad.

Here are some things you can do yourself to deal with the pressure of school.

1. WHAT ARE YOUR SKILLS?

Everyone has different interests, and different skills. You don't have to be good at everything, or enjoy everything – school is a great time to work out what you love, and what you excel at.

You'll still have to do the things you're not so good at, and it's important to work hard at them, but it can take the pressure off to remember you don't have to be brilliant at everything. Finding out what you enjoy helps too; normally, the more you enjoy a subject or activity, the more often you want to do it, the more you get out of it, and the more you achieve.

Try not to compare yourself to others too much. Everyone is good at different things, and you don't need to look at your skills compared with other people's.

Everyone is a differently shaped peg in a world of differently shaped holes. There are are jobs and opportunities out there for you whatever your skills – you don't have to force yourself to fit into a differently shaped hole.

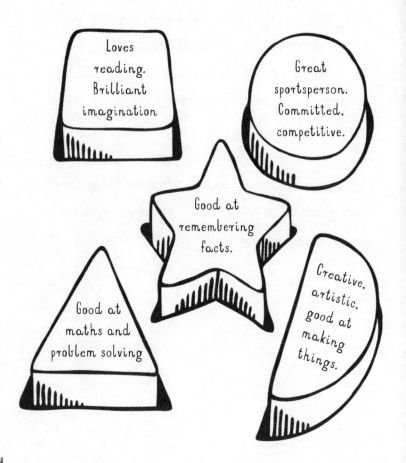

Loves reading. Brilliant imagination

Great sportsperson. Committed, competitive.

Good at remembering facts.

Good at maths and problem solving

Creative, artistic, good at making things.

2. BE ORGANIZED

School is more hectic and stressful if you're not ready for it. There is a lot to remember – books for each lesson, equipment, sports kit, permission slips, homework on the right days and so on. Don't expect yourself to be some kind of superhero and remember all those things off the top of your head. Take the pressure off by writing it all down.

Make use of your school planner, or get a diary to keep track of everything. Write down exactly what your homework is and when it is due. Get things ready in your bag the night before, to avoid rushing around in the morning. If you look at your phone often, you could use the calendar there.

3. STAY ON TOP OF THINGS

As you get older, you'll probably get more and
more homework to do. Homework can feel like
a chore but learning to work independently
is an important part of education. The key to
reducing pressure on yourself is to stay on top of
the work you have to do.

Use your planner, and try to do homework
as soon as it's set. That way it'll be fresh in your
mind. Once it's done, you don't have to worry
about it!

If you can get into the habit of doing that
now, you'll be in a good position to keep tackling
it well when the workload gets heavier.

EXAMS

Whatever school you go to, at some point you're going to have to do some exams. Almost everyone finds exams stressful, so if the thought of them scares you, you're not alone.

There's no avoiding exams, but you can do a lot to make them as stress-free as possible – your mental health doesn't have to suffer because it's exam time. Here are some top tips for coping.

1. PLAN YOUR REVISION

It sounds obvious, but the more work you do, the more ready you'll be and the easier you'll find the exam. Give yourself plenty of time, and plan it in advance so you know you'll cover everything before the exam.

2. REVISE

Concentrate hard for short bursts, then take little breaks, so you don't get worn out.

Ask someone at home if they can test you, or work with one of your friends.

3. PREPARE

Find out what the exam will be like: is it short answers, essays, oral, practical? Get together the things you need for the exam itself - pens, pencils, rubber. For some you might need a calculator, ruler or maths equipment.

4. RELAX

Look after yourself and your mental health by eating lots of healthy food, getting some exercise and lots of sleep. The night before an exam, have a restful evening. If you try to cram information in your head, you'll probably find it hard to sleep. Trust that you've done the work and preparation. Don't worry if you don't sleep well though, it's natural to be nervous and you'll be OK even if you're tired.

RELAXATION TIPS

Relaxing sometimes is great for your physical and mental health. It can keep your stress levels down, helps you cope with things that come your way, and can even boost your memory to help with school work. (That doesn't mean just sleeping or watching TV all the time though... You don't get out of stuff that easily.)

To relax and unwind you could:

- Rest in a quiet room for a while. Teenage life is loud and busy — it's OK to take time out.
- Turn your phone off for a couple of hours.
- Go out and get some fresh air and a change of scene.
- Breathe. Take a deep breath in, and a deep breath out. Do it several times with your eyes closed. You can lie down to do it if you like. Feel the breath coming in and out, relaxing all of your body and slowing down any noisy or stressful thoughts.

- Try mindfulness. That's what psychologists call being aware of everything going on around you in the moment, using all your senses. Rather than worrying about a big thing coming up, focus completely on small things that are happening right now — what you can feel under your fingers, what you can hear, smell, taste and see, what textures are like, what temperature things are. Staying really focused on your physical surroundings for a short time can distract you from big thoughts or worries.

These are great tips for your daily life too, not just in the run-up to exams.

CHANGE

Your teenage years are likely to be full of change. You'll probably change school at some point, which might involve changing friendships too. You're in a period of change in your body, and, as you get older, what people expect of you alters as well.

Some people love change, embrace it, and enjoy all the new adventures and freedoms that getting older brings. But some people find it a little scary, and unnerving.

BIG SCARY NEW SCHOOL

I'm not ready for this...

You might not feel ready for those new things, or might like how your life is already and not want anything about it to be different.

Feeling either way is OK. Change can be great, and it can be nerve-wracking, but worrying about getting older and things changing won't stop them from happening.

When changes happen, it can take a while for them to settle down, but soon enough they'll feel normal, and you'll be used to it before you know it.

DRINK AND DRUGS

The new freedom that comes with getting older
and being a teenager also involves some risks and
decisions. As you take on more responsibility, it's
up to you to make choices that keep you safe,
rather than relying on adults such as your parents
or teachers to make those decisions for you.

Something you may hear people start to
talk about is drugs. 'Drugs' is a broad term for
chemicals that change how your brain and
body work. The term covers all sorts of things,
including medicines, illegal recreational drugs,
and legal things you might see around you a lot,
such as coffee, alcohol, and cigarettes.

Some drugs such as alcohol and cigarettes are
age-controlled, which means that although they
might be harmful, they are legal once you are
above a certain age.

Other drugs, such as tea, coffee and cola,
have no age laws, and are used by lots of people,

without many dangerous or negative effects. Used sensibly and within advised guidelines they're not a bad thing.

But just because some drugs are legal, doesn't mean they're harmless. All drugs have the potential to be addictive, which means people feel they need to have them, and suffer withdrawal symptoms if they don't. Alcohol, cigarettes and prescription drugs can be dangerous, misused and abused, and can lead to physical and mental illnesses.

Some drugs, including cocaine, cannabis, heroin and MDMA, are illegal in most countries. These are called 'recreational drugs', and are illegal because they are potentially very harmful and dangerous.

You might come across illegal or age-controlled drugs at some point, through friends, or older siblings. This can have a few consequences for your mental health.

1. PEER PRESSURE

You might feel pressure to try drink, drugs or cigarettes, if other people are and that pressure can make you feel miserable, confused, or insecure. You don't have to try them, even if people around you are, particularly if it's breaking the law. You always have the right to say no, however hard it feels.

THE LAW

Buying alcohol or cigarettes under the age of 18 is illegal in most countries. If the police find you with them you could be fined and/or given a criminal record.

Recreational drugs are illegal whatever age you are and possessing them is a serious crime.

2. MESSING WITH YOUR MIND

Alcohol and drugs change how your brain is working. Alcohol is a depressant – it slows down connections in the brain, and can make you feel sad and upset, even if you felt happy beforehand. If someone has a mental health problem it can make it worse.

Many drugs are stimulants, that have the opposite effect, and speed up connections in the brain. These can make you feel stressed, frantic and paranoid. There is also evidence that taking some recreational drugs can lead to long-term mental health problems.

Being addicted to a drug can also make you feel dependent, helpless, and trapped. Addiction can be a mental health problem in itself.

3. AFFECTING DECISIONS

Alcohol and recreational drugs lower your inhibitions, which means they make you more likely to do things you wouldn't otherwise do. You might take more risks, your traffic sense is likely to be poorer, and you're much more likely to have unprotected sex, or do something else you might regret.

4. YOUR PHYSICAL HEALTH

Many drugs can harm your body, and in turn affect your self-esteem and state of mind.

Cigarettes can severely damage your throat and lungs, while drinking a lot can harm your liver, as well as your developing brain.

If you think you, or someone you know, may be struggling with the effects of drugs or addiction, there are lots of places to go for help. You can talk to a counsellor at school, or a GP for help with all sorts of problems, and they will refer you to people or services that can help more. For links to websites with more advice and information, visit the Usborne Quicklinks website (see page 256).

PAUSE

The next section deals with some serious mental health problems. These are much less common than the negative feelings we all have from time to time, and not everyone will experience them in their lives.

But it's important to know a little about them, and be aware of what they are, in part so you know what to do if you think you're ever affected, but mostly so you can be kind and understanding to other people who are having problems.

11

MENTAL HEALTH PROBLEMS

LONG-TERM EMOTIONS

Life is full of ups and downs. There are great
parts, difficult parts, exciting parts – and
it's completely normal for your emotions to
chop and change a lot. It's normal to feel sad
sometimes, and it's definitely normal not always
to know how you're feeling.

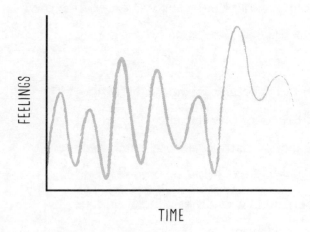

Sometimes though, for some people,
emotions don't come and go with what's
happening in life. Bad feelings, like sadness, anger

or worry, seem to stick, sometimes for months, or even years at a time.

When someone experiences these negative feelings for a long time, especially when those feelings aren't related specifically to what's going on in life at the time, it's called a mental health problem, or a mental illness. The problems are not all about being sad, though those are the most well-known. Mental health problems encompass all kinds of emotions and issues, and come in lots of forms. All mental health problems significantly affect the way someone thinks and feels.

Mental illnesses can be as damaging and scary as physical illnesses, and need to be taken just as seriously as physical illnesses.

HOW IS A MENTAL ILLNESS LIKE A BROKEN LEG?

That's not the start of a bad joke.

Physical illnesses and mental illnesses have a lot of things in common...

This person has a BROKEN ANKLE.

It hurts.

It's visible.

It needs medical attention.

It takes different people different amounts of time to get better.

It's clear where the pain or discomfort is, and the pain can be described.

...but they also differ in some crucial ways.
Spot the differences between these two people.

This person has a MENTAL ILLNESS.

It hurts.

It's
invisible.

It needs medical
attention.

It takes different
people different
amounts of time
to get better.

It can be hard to know
where, what or how it
hurts. It's difficult to
describe or explain.

WHAT'S THE CAUSE?

Mental health problems tend to occur when
certain networks and circuits in the brain don't
function normally. But what causes that unusual
functioning is a mystery. No one knows precisely
what causes most mental health problems
– they're extremely complicated, and most
conditions that affect the brain are very hard to
understand. Often there's no real cause at all.

Doctors think mental health problems might
be influenced by someone's experiences and
someone's genes (the information inside their
body's cells that makes them unique, inherited
from their parents.)

Having someone else in your family with a
mental health problem might mean that you're
more likely to get one, just like some physical
conditions, but that's not always the case.

Experiences that can sometimes trigger a
mental health problem include bereavements,

trauma, accidents and stress. But that's not always the case.

Everyone has different genes and everyone responds to their life experiences differently, and there is no set recipe for developing a mental health problem.

One thing's certain though: having a mental health problem does not mean the person is weak, or stupid, or isn't dealing with life well enough.

QUICK
QUIZ

Which of these reasons could cause someone to suffer
from a mental health problem? Pick any you think
are right.

- Being oversensitive
- Catching it from someone contagious
- Having a bad hair day
- Being too weak to fight it off
- Being pooed on by a bird
- Watching a sad movie
- Not being vaccinated against it
- Being a bad person
- Spilling tomato sauce on your jeans

The answer is NONE OF THESE. You can't catch a mental illness in
the way that you can catch a physical illness, and it's not a case of
being weak or oversensitive.

CHALLENGING STIGMA

In the past, doctors and the public weren't so understanding about mental health problems. Over time, people have thought some pretty terrible things about mental health problems, and how to treat them.

Ancient Greek cure: starving or beating

Ancient Indian cure: shocking the mental illness out of someone, by frightening or shaking them.

The fact that people have held these opinions in the past, means not everyone feels comfortable talking about mental health problems, and for some people there's still a negative judgement attached to mental health problems, called a stigma. This can put people off discussing it, but talking about mental health problems is really important, and helps a lot of people get better.

GETTING BETTER

The normal methods and strategies that people use to try to feel better when they feel sad or anxious don't always work for long-term mental health problems.

Usually, people with mental health problems need help from mental health specialists called psychiatrists and psychologists. Psychologists mostly look at the way someone acts on the things they feel, while psychiatrists look at how someone's body and brain are working.

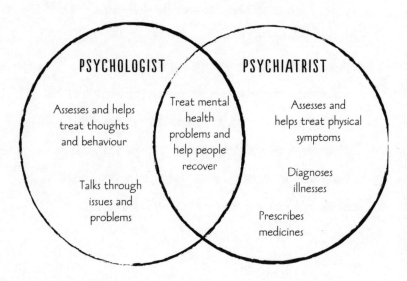

PSYCHOLOGIST

Assesses and helps treat thoughts and behaviour

Talks through issues and problems

Treat mental health problems and help people recover

PSYCHIATRIST

Assesses and helps treat physical symptoms

Diagnoses illnesses

Prescribes medicines

The type of medical treatment people receive depends on the type of mental illness they have, and different treatments work for different people.

Doctors often recommend a treatment called counselling, also known as therapy. Counselling comes in a number of forms, but essentially it's about discussing worries, fears and stresses. Some counselling helps get to the bottom of why those worries exist, and other counselling gives coping mechanisms and strategies to deal with the worries day-to-day. Both are able to change the circuits in the brain that aren't working quite right, and make someone feel better.

Some people are prescribed medicines. Others use a combination of medicine and counselling. Usually, counsellors and doctors work together to find the best course of treatment for each person.

12.

DEPRESSION AND ANXIETY

DEPRESSION

One of the mental health problems you'll probably hear people talking about the most is depression. Depression is a kind of deep sadness or emptiness that stays around for a long time – for weeks or longer.

People with depression tend to feel very 'low' – sad, miserable, unmotivated and extremely tired, though not everyone feels the same, and depression has a wide range of symptoms. Depression has a big impact on someone's life.

OVERWHELMED

MISERABLE

 **DARK**

LOW

Blue TIRED

SAD EMPTY

SADNESS VS DEPRESSION

People talk about being 'depressed', or things being 'depressing' a lot. Normally they actually mean they're feeling a little sad, or even just bored.

> Urgh! I hate Mondays. They're so depressing.

> I feel depressed just looking at it.

But sadness and depression are very different things. Everyone feels sad sometimes: when something goes wrong; when watching a sad film, or maybe on a Monday morning. Sadness is a temporary thing, that comes and goes, and is caused by something in particular (such as the weekend being over). By Tuesday, things are usually better.

Depression isn't temporary, and it doesn't always relate to what's going on in life. People with depression do tend to feel sad, but it's also much more than that.

WHAT DOES DEPRESSION FEEL LIKE?

Depression is not the same for everyone – everyone feels slightly different and there's no 'right' way to feel it. Here are some metaphors that explain how it feels to some people.

A dark cloud hanging over you.

Constantly swimming, trying to keep your head above water.

Blackness or nothingness

Something squeezing your chest and head all the time.

SQUEEZE

PRESS

SQUIDGE

WHAT DOCTORS LOOK FOR

Though depression feels different to everyone,
doctors have a set of criteria to help with
diagnosis. The criteria include:

- Feeling continually low and hopeless
- Losing enjoyment and interest in things
- Feeling grumpy or irritable a lot of the time
- Being tearful and upset
- Feeling constantly exhausted
- Having trouble sleeping or sleeping too much
- Not being able to concentrate
- Having no appetite or eating too much
- Losing perspective on things

The symptoms have to be around for at least
two weeks to be part of a depression diagnosis.

Though depression is commonly thought of
as a type of sadness, for some people, especially
children, that might not be the case. Young

people may be very irritable or become isolated, rather than being typically 'sad'.

INSIDE THE BRAIN

Scientists don't know exactly what's happening in the brain of a person with depression. It's likely to have something to do with the neurotransmitter

serotonin.

The tablets that doctors prescribe to treat depression help more serotonin pump through the brain, and for many people that does help. But the exact workings of depression are still a mystery to scientists.

What depression can feel like

WHAT DOES DEPRESSION LOOK LIKE?

Though depression is very difficult to cope with, and is often painful, there are not usually many external signs that someone is suffering, and people don't often broadcast it.

I'M DEPRESSED!

People don't tend to do this.

There's no bandage or bruise.

Sign my cast!

Um... sign my brain?

Sometimes depression *can* be spotted because someone stops caring for their appearance, avoids friends, or loses or puts on weight, but often there are no signs at all.

Anyone can get depressed. Being depressed doesn't mean someone is weak, or pathetic, or not trying hard enough. It just means they don't have enough of certain chemicals firing in their brains to make them feel happy. Similarly, being popular, rich, or good at things doesn't mean someone *can't* be depressed. It isn't related to how 'good' someone's life seems from the outside.

Some very famous people have talked about their struggles with depression. Winston Churchill, who was Prime Minister of Great Britain during the Second World War, used to describe his depression as a big black dog that was with him wherever he went.

JK Rowling, the author of the Harry Potter books, included characters called dementors that represented *her* experience of depression. She wrote "...they drain peace, hope and happiness out of the air around them. Get too near a dementor and every good feeling, every happy memory will be sucked out of you."

People who can be affected by depression:

RICH PEOPLE

POPULAR PEOPLE

FAMOUS PEOPLE

QUEENS

FOOTBALLERS

Singers

PRINCES

TEACHERS

SURGEONS

SUPERSTARS

ASTRONAUTS

NATIONAL TREASURES

ACTORS

PLUMBERS

OLD PEOPLE

YOUNG PEOPLE

WHAT TO DO

Just because anyone *could* get depression, it doesn't mean you will. Many people go through their lives without ever experiencing it.

But if you do ever think you might be depressed, the most important thing you can do is talk to someone about it. It's an illness that is tough to cope with, and can make you feel very lonely. The temptation is to stay on your own, and not to bother or burden anybody with the information.

You might worry that telling someone would make them feel bad or you think they might not take you seriously. Those are completely normal and natural concerns that a lot of people have, but most people find talking about it, and letting someone else know, lifts some of the weight off their shoulders.

WHO TO TALK TO

- A parent or carer
- A teacher at school
- Friends
- A doctor

Family and teachers may suggest you talk to a doctor. It's really important to get help from someone as soon as possible. They will talk to you about what is wrong, and can help you find the best way to get better.

A teacher or doctor will normally treat what you say as confidential, and keep it between you and them, unless you want others to know. But if someone thinks you're in real danger, they might have to pass the information on to a mental health professional, who will be able to help you quickly.

IF A FRIEND IS DEPRESSED

At some point in your life, you might come across someone who has depression, maybe a family member, a friend, or someone at school.

It can be hard to know what to do to make another person feel better – in fact, there's nothing you can do that will make them completely better. Remember their illness is not your fault, and you're not responsible for making other people better. All you can do is to listen – when someone has depression, talking about it will feel very difficult, but will also be very helpful. You don't have to solve the problem, but just being there for a chat will be a great help. You can remind a friend who has depression that there are adults they can talk to if they don't feel safe.

Being aware of depression, and knowing a little about it, will help you to understand other people. Everyone has hard times, especially during puberty, and lots of people are dealing with challenges you might not see on the outside. As you grow up, it's important you are as kind and supportive about illnesses that you can't see, as illnesses that you can.

THINGS NOT TO SAY:

Though you might not know what to say, there are some things NOT to say to someone you think is depressed:

"Cheer up!"

This is probably one of the most common things people say, and is one of the least helpful. If people could just cheer up they would.

"What've you got to be depressed about?"

Whether or not someone gets depression is irrespective of what you see as the quality of their life. The rich, popular, talented, famous – they can all get depression.

"You'll get over it."

Yes, hopefully they will get better. But this phrase belittles what someone might be going through, and will probably make them feel worse.

TRY THIS...

If you are feeling really down or depressed, here are some little things that might help:

- Talk. To family, friends, your dog, a toy you had when you were little, or even just into your phone. Saying your feelings out loud can give you some relief.
- Go out for a walk in the fresh air.
- Draw, doodle or do something crafty. Doing something with your hands can be a good distraction from negative thoughts.
- Read a book. Don't worry if you can't concentrate completely on it, you could just dip in and out.
- Spend some quality time with a parent, sibling or friend. You might not feel like it, but it might help you feel connected, and remind you how much people value you.
- Do something nice for someone else — it'll distract you for a while, and make you feel good.

ANXIETY

Another common mental illness is called anxiety, where people feel particularly worried, scared and fearful.

Everyone feels anxious or nervous now and then, before an exam, a race, or meeting new people for example. But people with anxiety disorder feel anxious almost all the time, and worry significantly affects their lives. The worry can grab hold of anything – even if there's nothing scary or going wrong, the anxiety finds something to worry about.

SCARED

Sweat

PANIC

ANXIOUS

DREAD

WORRIED

Fear

NERVOUS

INSIDE THE BRAIN

When people are anxious, their bodies are full of

ADRENALINE

Adrenaline has a lot of physical effects on the body. It makes the heart beat very hard and fast, makes breathing quick, and can make someone shaky and sweaty.

What anxiety can feel like

WHAT DOES ANXIETY FEEL LIKE?

Something heavy sitting on your chest making it hard to breathe.

People on your shoulders and in your brain shouting bad things at you all the time.

Something twisting your heart and all your insides.

SYMPTOMS OF ANXIETY

Below are the symptoms of anxiety that doctors look for. People tend to feel some of them almost all the time, for months on end.

Shortness of breath

Nightmares

Shaking

Difficulty swallowing

Sweating

Fidgeting

Feelings of dread

Headache

Tense muscles

Unable to sleep

Crying

TYPES OF ANXIETY

Anxiety comes in several forms. Here are some types that most affect young people:

- **GENERALIZED ANXIETY** – worrying excessively about anything and everything, including school, exams, family, friends and health.
- **SEPARATION ANXIETY** – this mostly affects young children, but teenagers can get it too. People with separation anxiety find it hard to leave parents or carers, and feel very nervous being without them.
- **SOCIAL ANXIETY** – this is the most common type of anxiety for teenagers. It's when normal nervousness about going out, answering the phone, or seeing other people becomes very intense and overwhelming.

Do I have to go outside? That's where the people are...

CALM-DOWN TOOLKIT

Some people with anxiety find having a box full of things
to distract all their senses can help them calm down.

SMELL

Freshly washed clothes, a blanket
with lavender oil on it (or
another smell you find relaxing).

SOUND

Music you love listening to –
maybe an audiobook you can
lose yourself in for a while.

SIGHT

A book you loved from your childhood
that feels familiar and happy, or
some photos you like looking at.

TOUCH

Different textures to feel and
fiddle with, such as bubble
wrap, an old teddy bear,
fidget toys or squishy putty.

...but I just wanted to say I've been feeling really anxious and I need to ge...

I've been keeping these worries bottled up for a long time...

WHAT TO DO

Just as with depression, talking to people is really
important. Getting worries out into the world
is healthier than keeping them bottled up, in
the long run. If you're worried about telling
somebody, it might be easier to write your
worries down, or record them on a phone first.

It is really important to see a doctor if
you suspect you're suffering from an anxiety
disorder. They will be able to put you in touch
with people who can help, who can give you

coping techniques and talk through your worries
(see pages 198-199). They might then give you
medicines that help, but taking medication will
be discussed with you first, so you'll never end up
taking something you don't want.

lk to someone about it all before I explode from holding them all inside me

TRY THIS

If you're at home, lie on the floor or on your bed.
Breathe in counting slowly to three, then out again,
counting slowly to three. Tense your toes for a few
seconds, then relax them. Tense your legs, then relax
them. Carry on all the way up your body, one part at a
time, tensing and relaxing, all
the time breathing slowly.

IF A FRIEND HAS ANXIETY

Someone with anxiety needs people around them to be patient and understanding. Things that are easy for you, such as walking to the shops, might be really hard for them. That means life tends to be quite exhausting for someone with anxiety.

The best thing you can do is reassure a friend who has anxiety that they're not being silly, that you understand, and that everything is going to be OK, even if it doesn't feel OK right now.

You could support someone by going with them to the shops or to a party if they're nervous, and sticking with them. Or you could challenge them to do something they're scared of, then share a treat.

Remember, it's not your job or responsibility to fix someone or make them better. If anxiety is having a serious impact on someone's life, that person needs to go and get professional help from a doctor.

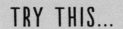
TRY THIS...

If you or anyone you know is feeling very anxious, you could try one of these. Not everything works for everyone, so try a range and see what's effective for you.

- Take a shower — imagine the worries washing away with the water.
- Go for a short walk or run. Anxiety can make you feel like you have a lot of restless energy.
- Scribble on, scrunch or tear a piece of paper.
- Keep a worry box. Write down the thing you're worrying about, and put it in an old shoe box or tissue box. Add things to the box when you need to get them out of your head.
- Write down a list of things you're looking forward to, to get you out of the panicked-right-now feeling.
- Take time out on your own. Lie down, breathe, and relax your muscles, until the worries ebb away.

Eating Disorders

13.

FUELLING YOUR BODY

Bodies need energy to do absolutely everything
– for your heart to beat, your legs to walk,
your arms to move. Your brain needs energy
just to think. That means every day your body
burns through lots of fuel, and that fuel needs
replacing. You need to eat enough every
day to keep all those processes going, and
need *extra* fuel during puberty to grow and
develop healthily.

For some people, eating the right amount
each day is very difficult. There is a whole
group of mental health problems to do with
food, known as eating disorders.

EATING DISORDERS

Eating disorders are serious illnesses, during which worries about food take over people's lives. People with eating disorders have a very negative relationship with food, and their eating habits and behaviour are controlled by the disorder.

Scientists don't know exactly what causes eating disorders. For some people, it's an extension of anxiety or depression, and cutting down on food is a way for someone to feel punished, or ease their guilt.

For some people, eating disorders begin as a way of finding control in a chaotic life – they can control what, when and how often they eat, when they can't control other things.

Other people looking in from the outside may envy that person's 'self-control' if they are missing snacks, or eating only small meals. But it's not the person with the disorder that has control – eating disorders take over and control every aspect of that person's life, and make it miserable. Like an alien takeover, only not in science-fiction, and much worse.

Eating disorder in control

BODY DYSMORPHIC DISORDER

Body dysmorphic disorder, known as BDD, is a type of anxiety disorder related to body image. It is common in people with eating disorders, but it can exist on its own as well. People with BDD don't see themselves as everyone else sees them. Things they think are problems with their appearance look really big and obvious to them, while everyone else might not notice any problem at all.

IN THE MIRROR

Someone with BDD does not see what others see when they look in the mirror. From the outside, you might think the person looks really good, but they can only see the negatives, which are exaggerated and feel overwhelming. They can't imagine that you don't see those flaws, however many times you say so.

Everyone feels down on themselves sometimes, and everyone has moments when they don't feel they look good, but, for someone with BDD, those thoughts are almost constant, and have a big impact on their life. Reassurance and compliments don't usually help either, so it can be hard to make someone feel better.

Though it's easy to get frustrated, people with BDD are not being attention-seeking, vain, or obsessed with their looks. They are consumed by negative thoughts, and often have depression or anxiety as well. They need professional help and support, just like people with other mental health problems (see Chapters 11 and 12).

BINGE EATING DISORDER

Binge eating disorder, or BED, is a disorder where people eat a large amount of food very quickly, in what is known as a 'binge'. Everyone sometimes eats more than they need, at parties, or on special occasions, but people with binge eating disorder do it regularly, and compulsively (they feel like they have to).

Binge eating often happens in secret, so it's hard to know if someone suffers from this disorder, unless they tell you.

People with binge eating disorder run the risk of developing phsyical health problems such as high blood pressure and high cholesterol, and some people are affected by diabetes. As with all eating disorders, it often comes hand-in-hand with anxiety or depression.

BULIMIA

One of the most common eating disorders
is bulimia nervosa. People with bulimia are in
a cycle of bingeing, then getting rid of the
food from their bodies in a process known as
purging – vomiting, or taking medicines called
laxatives that make you poo. Sometimes people
purge by exercising in an extreme way too. This
destructive cycle usually happens every day, and
can go on for months, or years.

After bingeing, people with bulimia tend to
feel extremely guilty, and are often filled with
self-hatred. It's a vicious circle, and often comes
with depression and anxiety (see Chapter 12).

The bulimia vicious cycle:

It seems to include a lot of feeling bad...

EFFECTS OF BULIMIA

Bulimia is extremely damaging to someone's health. Vital nutrients are lost every time someone purges, so people with bulimia can end up being malnourished and physically ill.

When someone makes themselves sick, it brings up acid up from the stomach, eroding teeth, irritating the throat, and causing bad breath. The physical effects of bulimia can include:

Weakness and tiredness

Sore throat

Poor hair and skin condition

Bad breath

Damaged teeth

Vomiting regularly can have a dangerous effect on the balance of substances called electrolytes in someone's body. Electrolyte imbalances can cause someone's heart to beat irregularly, can cause kidney damage and are generally extremely dangerous.

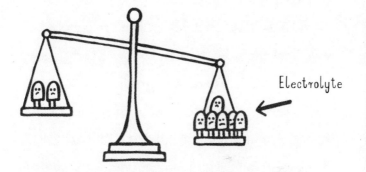

Electrolyte

Though people with bulimia are often malnourished, that doesn't mean they're always thin. You can't tell whether someone has an eating disorder by looking at them – eating disorders are about someone's behaviour, and how their lives are dictated by food, not how big or small they are.

ANOREXIA

Anorexia nervosa is probably the most well-known eating disorder, even if it is not the most common. People with anorexia try to keep their weight as low as possible, often starving themselves or exercising a dangerous amount in order to lose weight.

Anorexia is a controlling illness – people who feel the need to monitor everything they consume can't take part in group meals, go to cafés, restaurants or parties with friends or family, or enjoy trips or holidays. It's extremely destructive and ends up affecting every aspect of someone's life.

EFFECTS OF ANOREXIA

Anorexia can take a huge toll on someone's physical health. By starving themselves, people with anorexia do not give their bodies the essential nutrients they need to function, grow and repair. This is particularly problematic during puberty when bodies need extra fuel to develop and form new brain connections (see page 15). The physical effects of anorexia can include:

Being extremely cold

Hair thinning or falling out

Dizziness or fainting

Growing thicker body hair to keep the body warm

Painful joints and bones

Anorexia is an extremely serious condition, and physical effects can be severe and long-lasting. It can permanently weaken people's bones, giving them a condition called osteoporosis. Having low body fat can also affect people's ability to make or have a baby, which might not feel like a problem as a teenager, but could really affect someone later in life. Ultimately, people can become so malnourished that their bodies start to shut down, and it can be fatal.

In fact, of all the mental health problems in this book, anorexia causes the death of the most people. It is not desirable, cool, fashionable, or attractive. It is miserable, lonely and extremely dangerous.

WHAT NOT TO SAY

It can be very hard to know what to say or how to help someone with anorexia. It is not your responsibility to solve the problem, but it might be useful to know what is particularly UNhelpful to say to someone:

- "Just eat more."
- "You've eaten a lot today."
- "Come on, eat up."
- "You don't look that thin."

HELPING

There's not much you can do on your own to help someone with anorexia. On the whole, the best thing to do is not to mention food at all. If they're eating – great. Don't draw attention to it. If they're not, telling them to eat more is probably not going to help.

Actually, that goes for everyone, not just people with eating disorders. Commenting on what or how much other people eat can make them feel self-conscious, ashamed, or guilty, and can create negative associations with food. Being relaxed around food is the most helpful thing you can do, to remind people that eating is normal, essential and for most people, really enjoyable.

Whatever you do, remember it's not your job to make anyone better. Someone with an eating disorder needs urgent professional medical help.

OTHER ISSUES

Though body dysmorphic disorder, binge eating disorder, bulimia and anorexia are the most common mental health problems associated with image and eating, there are some others.

Orthorexia is the name given to a condition where people are unhealthily obsessed with healthy living. They cut out certain foods that they believe aren't 'clean', 'pure' or healthy, and feel very guilty if they eat something they don't normally allow. It's not currently recognized as an eating disorder, but it makes behaviour obsessive and controlled, just as with eating disorders.

Another serious issue is exercise addiction. Many people with anorexia and bulimia exercise obsessively to keep their weight low, or to compensate for bingeing, but you can be addicted to exercise without having a diagnosed eating disorder as well.

People with an exercise addiction are physically active to an unhealthy degree, and feel they *have* to exercise. It can be to do with trying to lose weight, but for many it is a method of managing guilt or self-hatred. People might use exercise to punish themselves, or to justify what they've eaten or done in a day. For many people, an exercise addiction is a symptom of another mental health condition, such as depression.

PANT
PANT

WHAT TO DO

If you think you might be suffering from any of these disorders, there is help out there.

The most important person to contact is your doctor. Your GP will be able to talk to you and assess how you can best be helped, then will probably refer you to a psychologist or psychiatrist. They will be able to give you coping mechanisms, and step-by-step plans to help you become healthier. They can also address underlying issues that might be causing an eating disorder.

It is common for people with eating disorders to suffer from depression or anxiety as well, and psychologists and psychiatrists can also help you treat those conditions too (see pages 198-199).

There are charities and organizations that support people with eating disorders, and their family and friends too. For links to websites with advice about what to do about eating disorders and where to go for help, visit the Usborne Quicklinks website (see page 256).

If you're worried about talking to someone, it can help to write it down. Write down your worries through a day, how you've acted on those worries, and how you felt. That can help a family member or doctor understand what you're going through, spot any unhealthy behaviours, and help you find the best support to get better.

NO PROBLEM TOO SMALL

You might recognize some of the thoughts and feelings in this chapter, but feel like you don't have a problem serious enough to go and get help.

It's a good idea to go and get help even if you don't think you're *really* sick – the earlier you go and get support for negative thoughts about food, the quicker and easier getting better will be. One of the cruellest things about eating disorders is people suffering from them often don't realize they are sick, or underestimate just how ill they are. Having negative thoughts about food, over-eating, under-eating, or using food or exercise as a punishment, are all extremely unhealthy, and need urgent medical attention.

14

FINDING HELP

WHERE TO GO

If any of the problems in this book are affecting your life, it's a good idea to go and ask for help. Asking for help doesn't make you weak, pathetic, or unable to cope – it takes courage, and is a brave thing to do.

This chapter will list the people you could ask for help, where to find them, and some tips on how to go about it. They might not all suit you – that's OK, you'll probably feel more comfortable with some than others.

Things you might want to get help with include:

- Feeling sad, miserable or alone a lot
- Feeling panicky and anxious, or overwhelmed with worry
- Struggling to eat enough, or eating too much
- Difficulty concentrating

SOMEONE AT HOME

Your first port of call is likely to be someone you live with at home – maybe a parent, carer, or other family member. They probably know you well and should listen to what you tell them. Adults in your family will be able to support you, or go with you to find professional help if you need it. There are many problems you'll probably be able to work out together, without going to get more help.

If you're worried about telling a family member, or not sure what to say, try writing your worries or problems down on a piece of paper. That can help you work out what you're really feeling, and you can always give them the piece of paper rather than talking out loud, if you find that easier.

SCHOOL

If you're unsure about telling your family, or the problem is related to issues at home, you could talk to a teacher, counsellor or other staff member at school.

This is especially useful if the problem is to do with school, for example if you're being bullied, or if you are very anxious about your work.

Most schools have counsellors or nurses who can help you with problems you might be having. They can give you practical advice for coping in school, and direct you to any other services that may be of use.

MEDICAL HEALTH PROFESSIONALS

Your family, school counsellor or teacher might recommend that you go and see a medical health professional. These are doctors, psychologists and psychiatrists.

Your local doctor is a good person to go and talk to. You probably already have a doctor that you've visited as a child, and you can talk to them about mental health as well as physical health – they're trained to help with both. A doctor can prescribe you medicines to help with depression or anxiety if they think it's appropriate. This will be discussed with you beforehand. Your doctor might also refer you to other professionals, who are specialists in mental health: psychologists or psychiatrists.

MENTAL HEALTH SERVICES

You don't always have to go through a doctor to been seen by a psychologist or psychiatrist. A lot of towns and cities have dedicated mental health services, including clinics and walk-ins. For some of them you need to have a referral from a doctor or make an appointment, but for others you can just walk in. It's these specialist local services that your doctor will probably refer you to, and they offer therapy such as counselling, where you discuss how you're feeling, or where those feelings come from. They also usually offer a treatment called CBT - cognitive behavioural therapy. CBT is all about finding ways to cope with the thoughts and feelings you have, and finding practical solutions to help make your life easier and happier.

For more about counselling and the difference between psychologists and psychiatrists, go to page 198.

TOP TIPS FOR TALKING ABOUT YOUR MENTAL HEALTH

- If you're nervous, try using a text or letter first, before talking face to face. You could use bullet points, or draw, if that's easier.

- Think about the feelings and thoughts you've had, and how they affected you. For example, if you felt really anxious so you couldn't eat your dinner, or if you were so worried that you felt sick. This can help you explain and describe what you're experiencing.

- Be as open and honest as you can. It's OK to be vague, or to not really know how you feel, but the more you say, the more likely it is someone else will be able to help.

- Don't think you've failed by asking for help. Recognizing that you're allowed to get help, and you are worth the help you receive, is a really important part of feeling better.

IF SOMEONE ELSE TALKS TO YOU ABOUT THEIR MENTAL HEALTH

Sometimes other people such as your friends or family members might talk to you about problems they're having or difficult thoughts they're experiencing. It's not very easy to hear that someone you care about is having trouble. Here are some tips for if someone talks to you about their mental health problems:

- Firstly, remember it's not your responsibility to make them better. There are plenty of people out there who can make them better; you're just there to be a sounding board and good friend.

- Don't try to offer solutions immediately. There aren't always easy ways out, and it can be frustrating to hear someone try to solve the problem.

- Instead, listen carefully. Don't interrupt, or talk over the person sharing with you. They might not find it easy to talk about it, so give them time and be patient.

- Don't start gossiping about that person, or being rude about them behind their back. It took a lot of courage to share with you, and you should respect that.

- Advise them to go and talk to an adult, either at home or school, who will be able to help.

- Don't think it's your fault. People get mental health problems for all sorts of reasons, usually due to the chemicals in their brains, or experiences they've had. It's not because you haven't been a good enough friend, sibling, son or daughter.

USBORNE QUICKLINKS

There are loads of useful resources online that can help you with your mental health, from relaxation exercises and exam tips, to information on all sorts of mental health problems. For links to these sites and more, go to www.usborne.com/quicklinks, and type in the keywords 'mental health'.

Glossary

Here are some definitions of terms used through the book.
Words in bold have their own entries.

ADDICTION – physical or mental dependence on a substance or an activity. Common substance addictions include nicotine, alcohol and recreational drugs. Activity addictions can include gambling or playing video games.

AGENDER – a **gender** identity where someone does not identify with any gender.

ANOREXIA NERVOSA – an **eating disorder** in which someone continues to believe that they need to be thinner, no matter what size they are. People with anorexia have a significantly low weight, and often starve themselves or deliberately over-exercise in order to lose weight.

ANXIETY – a **mental health problem** characterized by overwhelming worry, fear or stress.

ASEXUALITY – a **sexuality** where someone does not experience physical sexual attraction.

BINGE EATING – eating a lot at once, much past the point of being full up.

BINGE EATING DISORDER (BED) – an **eating disorder**, that involves compulsively **binge eating**.

BIPOLAR DISORDER – a **mental health problem** that causes extreme mood swings over long periods of time. Someone with bipolar disorder experiences 'manic', high periods followed by very low periods of **depression**.

BISEXUALITY – a **sexuality** where someone experiences attraction to people of more than one **gender**.

BODY DYSMORPHIC DISORDER (BDD) – someone with BDD has an altered perception of themselves, and a very negative **body image**. BDD often comes hand-in-hand with **eating disorders** and other **mental health problems** such as **depression**.

BODY IMAGE – the way that someone sees themselves and how they feel about their body.

BORDERLINE PERSONALITY DISORDER (BPD) – a **mental health problem** in which someone has difficulty regulating and responding to their **emotions**. It can look very different in different people: some people experience very extreme emotions that change very quickly, some people act impulsively or dangerously, and some people feel empty or lonely.

BRAIN – the organ that sits inside your skull, and controls all your movement, bodily functions, thoughts and **emotions**.

BULIMIA — an **eating disorder** in which someone **binge eats**, and then purges the food from their body by making themselves sick or taking tablets called laxatives which make them poo.

BULLYING — hurting, intimidating or mocking someone, through physical, verbal or online abuse.

CHROMOSOMES — X-shaped structures found in body cells. Every cell in each person's body contains the same chromosomes, including **sex** chromosomes called X and/or Y chromosomes, that determine that person's sex.

CISGENDER — a **gender** identity that is the same as the **sex** someone was assigned at birth.

CONTRACEPTION — physical and/or **hormonal** methods of stopping someone becoming pregnant through sex, including condoms and the pill.

CONSENT — express permission, particularly for sexual activity. No one should have sex without all individuals giving consent, and consent can be withdrawn at any time, including during sex.

COUNSELLING — a kind of talking therapy where someone discusses their problems, fears and stresses with a professional. It's a key part of recovery from a **mental health problem**.

CYBERBULLYING — **bullying** someone through a phone, computer or tablet, generally on **social media**.

DEPRESSION – a mental health problem characterized by feelings of sadness, lowness, or emptiness, over at least 2 weeks. Depression can affect someone's ability to enjoy the things they usually would, and can stop them functioning normally.

DIET – all the food that someone eats day-to-day. It can also mean a set of foods restricted in some way to help someone lose or gain weight, or become healthier, but this kind of diet should only be followed with the advice of a doctor or nutritionist.

DISABILITY – a medical condition that affects someone's body, **brain** or senses. It may affect or impair someone's actions, movement or experience of the world.

DISCRIMINATION – unfair treatment of someone, due to something about them such as **gender**, race, **sexuality**, or **disability**.

EATING DISORDER – a group of **mental health problems** that negatively affect someone's relationship with food. The negative relationship usually dictates a lot of that person's life, and can end up damaging someone's **physical health** as well.

EMOTION – a strong feeling, for example happiness, sadness or anger. Emotions can be felt in someone's body as well as their **brain**.

FEMALE – if someone's **sex** is female, then they are usually born with two X **chromosomes**, and have female reproductive organs, including a vagina and uterus. Many people with female reproductive organs also identify with the **gender** 'woman' but this is not always the case.

GENDER – a term that some people use interchangeably with the word '**sex**', to mean whether someone is **male** or **female**. But someone's sex is determined by the physical characteristics they're assigned at birth, while their gender is how they identify, feel and act. Someone's gender and sex may be the same, or may be different.

GENDER DYSPHORIA – if someone experiences gender dysphoria, they feel extremely unhappy or distressed with the **sex** they were assigned at birth, and feel it doesn't match their **gender** identity.

GENDER FLUID – if someone is gender fluid, they have no fixed or permanent **gender** and may identify as different genders at different times.

HETEROSEXUALITY – a **sexuality** where someone experiences attraction to people of a different **gender**.

HOMOPHOBIA – negative attitudes and actions towards **homosexual** people, or anyone else in the **LGBTQ+** community. Homophobia can take many forms, including **discrimination**, and **bullying**.

HOMOSEXUALITY – a **sexuality** where someone experiences attraction to people of the same **gender**. This is also known as being gay.

HORMONE – a chemical messenger that travels through blood and lets parts of someone's body communicate with each other. Hormones can influence your **emotions**, and also affect changes that happen to your body during **puberty**.

INTERSEX – if someone is intersex, they are born with a variety of internal and external characteristics that do not fit exactly to the definitions of either '**male**' or '**female**'.

LESBIAN – a word sometimes used to describe a **homosexual** woman.

LGBTQ+ – stands for **lesbian**, gay, **bisexual**, **trans**, questioning (or queer) and others. It refers to people across the world united by having **genders** or **sexualities** that are different to the **heterosexual** and **cisgender** majority.

MALE – if someone's **sex** is male, then they are usually born with one X and one Y chromosome, and have male reproductive organs, including a penis and testicles. Many people with male reproductive organs also identify with the **gender** 'man' but this is not always the case.

MENTAL HEALTH – the wellbeing of someone's **brain**.

MENTAL HEALTH PROBLEM – a serious disorder that affects the way someone thinks, feels and acts, for a prolonged period of time. It can also be known as a mental health condition or mental illness.

NEUROTRANSMITTER – a chemical messenger that helps cells in someone's brain communicate. Neurotransmitters include dopamine and serotonin and play a part in **mental health**.

NON-BINARY – if someone is non-binary, they identify as any **gender** outside either 'male' or 'female'. This is also sometimes called 'genderqueer'.

OBSESSIVE COMPULSIVE DISORDER (OCD) – a serious **mental health problem** where persistent, unpleasant thoughts and urges make someone feel they have to complete a certain behaviour, or repeat actions over and over again in order to reduce **anxiety**.

PANGENDER – a **gender** identity where someone identifies with all genders.

PANSEXUALITY – a **sexuality** where someone experiences attraction to people of all **genders**.

PEER PRESSURE – the feeling of being influenced by others. Peer pressure can be a positive or negative thing, but is usually used to describe being led into things that might be harmful or dangerous, for example, drinking, taking drugs, or misbehaving.

PHYSICAL HEALTH – the wellbeing of someone's body.

PSYCHIATRIST – a **mental health** professional who specializes in assessing and treating the physical symptoms of a **mental health problem**. Psychiatrists are doctors who can diagnose illnesses and prescribe medicine to treat them.

PSYCHOLOGIST – a **mental health** professional who specializes in assessing and treating negative or harmful behaviour that can stem from a **mental health problem**, and can help talk through problems with **counselling**.

PUBERTY – the process of developing and growing up into an adult. During puberty, **hormones** cause someone's body to develop into its adult shape, usually capable of having children. At this time, the **brain** also rewires and forms lots of new connections. Puberty generally starts between ages 8 to 13 for **females**, and 9 to 15 for **males**.

QUEER – Some people use 'queer' as an umbrella term to refer to the whole **LGBTQ+** community. Some people use it to describe their own **sexuality** as simply 'not **heterosexual**'. For a long time the word queer was used as an insult, but it is now generally used by people in the queer community to encourage openness and support among sexual and **gender** minorities.

SCHIZOPHRENIA – a serious **mental health problem** in which someone finds it hard to work out what is real and what is inside their head. They might hear or see hallucinations, or experience very muddled and confusing thoughts.

SELF-ESTEEM – someone's opinion of themselves, and their worth and value.

SELF-HARM – the act of hurting or endangering oneself on purpose.

SEX – all the characteristics including physical organs and **chromosomes** that someone is born with, and that make them generally **male** or **female**. Someone's sex can be the same as, or different to, their **gender**.

SEXUALITY – someone's sexual identity, with regard to the **gender/s** of people they are attracted to.

SOCIAL MEDIA – applications and websites that allow people to network, connect and share content.

STEREOTYPE – a simplistic, often judgemental view of a type of person, that causes others to treat them a certain way or think certain things of them. Such views are usually inaccurate and can be damaging, for example thinking that all girls like pink and can't throw a ball.

STIGMA – a negative judgement surrounding a topic, that makes people unwilling to discuss the topic or open up about it.

SUICIDAL THOUGHTS – this is a very extreme aspect of **mental health problems** for some people. Suicidal feelings involve someone thinking about death, wanting to die, or planning how to end their life. Thoughts and feelings like this are extremely serious and if you ever experience them you should tell someone quickly. Go to the Usborne Quicklinks website for links to sites with numbers that you can call if you feel you need urgent help (see page 256).

TRANSGENDER OR TRANS – a **gender** identity that differs from the **sex** someone was assigned at birth. A transgender person may undergo surgery or **hormonal** treatment to align their body with their gender identity.

INDEX

NOTES